WORLD HISTORY SERIES ■ ■ ■

The Cold War

Titles in the World History Series

The Cold War

by
Britta Bjornlund

Lucent Books, an Imprint of The Gale Group,
10911 Technology Place, San Diego, CA 92127

Library of Congress Cataloging-in-Publication Data

Bjornlund, Britta S.
     The Cold War / by Britta Bjornlund.
          p.   cm.—(World history series)
     Includes bibliographical references and index.
     Summary: Discusses the origins of the Cold War and its ef-
fects on Europe, Asia, and the United States, nuclear threats,
détente, and the future of the relationship between Russia and
the United States.
          ISBN 1-59018-003-8 (hardback : alk. paper)
          1. Cold War—Juvenile literature.   2. World politics—
1945—Juvenile literature.   3. Nuclear warfare—Juvenile
literature.   4. Détente—Juvenile literature.   5. United
States—Foreign relations—Russia (Federation)—Juvenile
literature.   6. Russia (Federation)—Foreign relations—
United States—Juvenile literature.   [1. Cold War. 2. World
politics—1945– 3. Nuclear warfare. 4. Détente. 5. United
States—Foreign relations—Soviet Union. 6. Soviet Union—
Foreign relations—United States.]   I. Title. II. Series.
          D843 .B528 2002
          327' .09 ' 0045—dc21   2001004873

Copyright 2002 by Lucent Books, an Imprint of The Gale Group,
10911 Technology Place, San Diego, California 92127

Printed in the U.S.A.

Contents

Foreword

Each year on the first day of school, nearly every history teacher faces the task of explaining why his or her students should study history. One logical answer to this question is that exploring what happened in our past explains how the things we often take for granted—our customs, ideas, and institutions—came to be. As statesman and historian Winston Churchill put it, "Every nation or group of nations has its own tale to tell. Knowledge of the trials and struggles is necessary to all who would comprehend the problems, perils, challenges, and opportunities which confront us today." Thus, a study of history puts modern ideas and institutions in perspective. For example, though the founders of the United States were talented and creative thinkers, they clearly did not invent the concept of democracy. Instead, they adapted some democratic ideas that had originated in ancient Greece and with which the Romans, the British, and others had experimented. An exploration of these cultures, then, reveals their very real connection to us through institutions that continue to shape our daily lives.

Another reason often given for studying history is the idea that lessons exist in the past from which contemporary societies can benefit and learn. This idea, although controversial, has always been an intriguing one for historians. Those who agree that society can benefit from the past often quote philosopher George Santayana's famous statement, "Those who cannot remember the past are condemned to repeat it." Historians who subscribe to Santayana's philosophy believe that, for example, studying the events that led up to the major world wars or other significant historical events would allow society to chart a different and more favorable course in the future.

Just as difficult as convincing students to realize the importance of studying history is the search for useful and interesting supplementary materials that present historical events in a context that can be easily understood. The volumes in Lucent Books' World History Series attempt to present a broad, balanced, and penetrating view of the march of history. Ancient Egypt's important wars and rulers, for example, are presented against the rich and colorful backdrop of Egyptian religious, social, and cultural developments. The series engages the reader by enhancing historical events with these cultural contexts. For example, in *Ancient Greece*, the text covers the role of women in that society. Slavery is discussed in *The Roman Empire*, as well as how slaves earned their freedom. The numerous and varied aspects of everyday life in these and other societies are explored in each volume of the series. Additionally, the series covers the major political, cultural, and philosophical ideas as the torch of civilization is passed from ancient Mesopotamia and Egypt, through Greece, Rome, Medieval Europe, and other world cultures, to the modern day.

The material in the series is formatted in a thorough, precise, and organized manner. Each volume offers the reader a comprehensive and clearly written overview of an important historical event or period. The topic under discussion is placed in a broad, historical context. For example, The Italian Renaissance begins with a discussion of the High Middle Ages and the loss of central control that allowed certain Italian cities to develop artistically. The book ends by looking forward to the Reformation and interpreting the societal changes that grew out of the Renaissance. Thus, students are not only involved in an historical era, but also enveloped by the events leading up to that era and the events following it.

One important and unique feature in the World History Series is the primary and secondary source quotations that richly supplement each volume. These quotes are useful in a number of ways. First, they allow students access to sources they would not normally be exposed to because of the difficulty and obscurity of the original source. The quotations range from interesting anecdotes to farsighted cultural perspectives and are drawn from historical witnesses both past and present. Second, the quotes demonstrate how and where historians themselves derive their information on the past as they strive to reach a consensus on historical events. Lastly, all of the quotes are footnoted, familiarizing students with the citation process and allowing them to verify quotes and/or look up the original source if the quote piques their interest.

Finally, the books in the World History Series provide a detailed launching point for further research. Each book contains a bibliography specifically geared toward student research. A second, annotated bibliography introduces students to all the sources the author consulted when compiling the book. A chronology of important dates gives students an overview, at a glance, of the topic covered. Where applicable, a glossary of terms is included.

In short, the series is designed not only to acquaint readers with the basics of history, but also to make them aware that their lives are a part of an ongoing human saga. Perhaps they will then come to the same realization as famed historian Arnold Toynbee. In his monumental work, *A Study of History*, he wrote about becoming aware of history flowing through him in a mighty current, and of his own life "welling like a wave in the flow of this vast tide."

Important Dates in the History of The Cold War

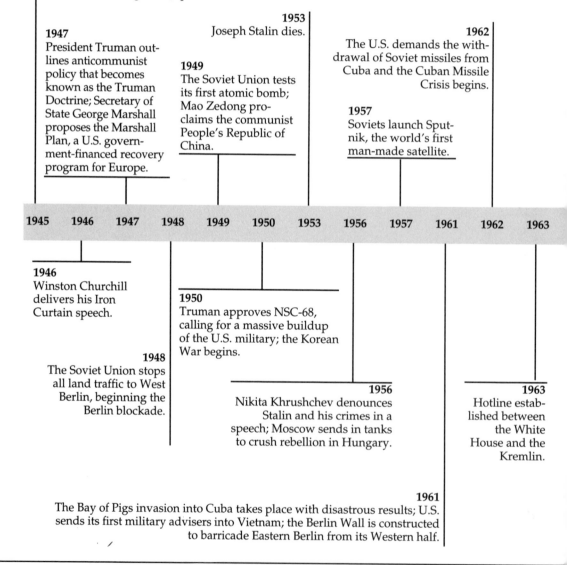

1945
Churchill, Roosevelt, and Stalin meet at Yalta Conference; leaders of Britain, the United States, and the Soviet Union meet at Potsdam Conference; U.S. drops atomic bombs on Hiroshima and Nagasaki, Japan.

1947
President Truman outlines anticommunist policy that becomes known as the Truman Doctrine; Secretary of State George Marshall proposes the Marshall Plan, a U.S. government-financed recovery program for Europe.

1953
Joseph Stalin dies.

1949
The Soviet Union tests its first atomic bomb; Mao Zedong proclaims the communist People's Republic of China.

1962
The U.S. demands the withdrawal of Soviet missiles from Cuba and the Cuban Missile Crisis begins.

1957
Soviets launch Sputnik, the world's first man-made satellite.

| 1945 | 1946 | 1947 | 1948 | 1949 | 1950 | 1953 | 1956 | 1957 | 1961 | 1962 | 1963 |

1946
Winston Churchill delivers his Iron Curtain speech.

1950
Truman approves NSC-68, calling for a massive buildup of the U.S. military; the Korean War begins.

1948
The Soviet Union stops all land traffic to West Berlin, beginning the Berlin blockade.

1956
Nikita Khrushchev denounces Stalin and his crimes in a speech; Moscow sends in tanks to crush rebellion in Hungary.

1963
Hotline established between the White House and the Kremlin.

1961
The Bay of Pigs invasion into Cuba takes place with disastrous results; U.S. sends its first military advisers into Vietnam; the Berlin Wall is constructed to barricade Eastern Berlin from its Western half.

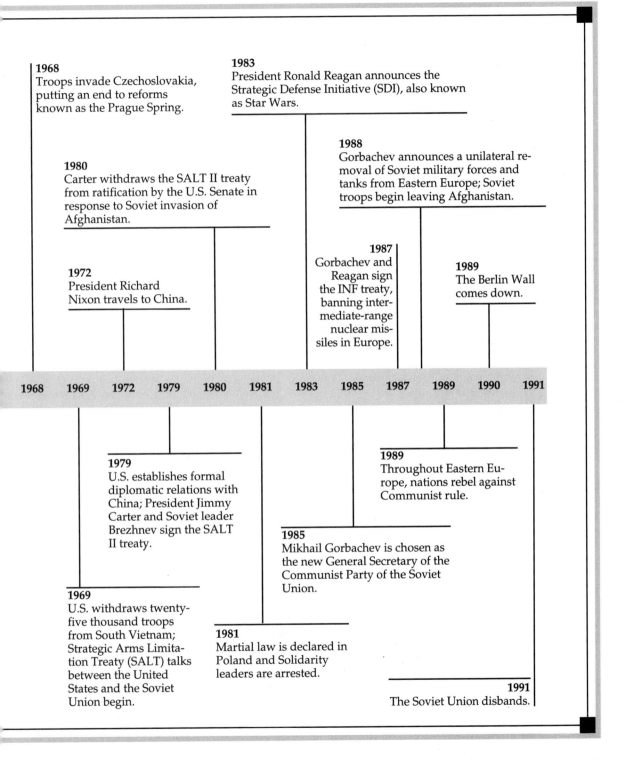

1968
Troops invade Czechoslovakia, putting an end to reforms known as the Prague Spring.

1983
President Ronald Reagan announces the Strategic Defense Initiative (SDI), also known as Star Wars.

1988
Gorbachev announces a unilateral removal of Soviet military forces and tanks from Eastern Europe; Soviet troops begin leaving Afghanistan.

1980
Carter withdraws the SALT II treaty from ratification by the U.S. Senate in response to Soviet invasion of Afghanistan.

1987
Gorbachev and Reagan sign the INF treaty, banning intermediate-range nuclear missiles in Europe.

1989
The Berlin Wall comes down.

1972
President Richard Nixon travels to China.

| 1968 | 1969 | 1972 | 1979 | 1980 | 1981 | 1983 | 1985 | 1987 | 1989 | 1990 | 1991 |

1979
U.S. establishes formal diplomatic relations with China; President Jimmy Carter and Soviet leader Brezhnev sign the SALT II treaty.

1989
Throughout Eastern Europe, nations rebel against Communist rule.

1985
Mikhail Gorbachev is chosen as the new General Secretary of the Communist Party of the Soviet Union.

1969
U.S. withdraws twenty-five thousand troops from South Vietnam; Strategic Arms Limitation Treaty (SALT) talks between the United States and the Soviet Union begin.

1981
Martial law is declared in Poland and Solidarity leaders are arrested.

1991
The Soviet Union disbands.

What Was the Cold War?

From the end of World War II in 1945 until the collapse of the Soviet Union in the early 1990s, international tensions engulfed the world in an ideological conflict known as the Cold War. The Cold War reflected po-

litical, economic, military, and cultural differences between the world's two superpowers, the Soviet Union and the United States. For more than forty-five years, their power struggle shaped the course of world

Two men help destroy the Berlin Wall. The fall of the Wall in November, 1989 was one event that marked the end of the Cold War.

events. It had major social, political, and economic effects on countries in every corner of the globe. Though the Cold War never took the form of sustained armed combat between the United States and the Soviet Union, both backed and participated in regional conflicts in Korea, Vietnam, and Afghanistan, with varying success. In these and other countries, the United States and the Soviet Union competed to spread their political views and expand their spheres of influence. In addition, both countries developed and stockpiled nuclear weapons in an unprecedented arms race that threatened the entire planet with nuclear destruction.

Throughout much of the twentieth century, an "iron curtain" seemed to divide the world between East, represented by the Soviet Union, and West, represented by the United States. In the late 1980s, however, this curtain began to lift. Soviet troops, once stationed in Eastern European nations to safeguard communism, made plans to withdraw. As a result, popular uprisings broke out and ousted Communist Party leaders. Massive demonstrations on both sides of Germany's Berlin Wall, which had separated East and West Berlin for over twenty-five years, led to the Wall's destruction in 1989. Later, in 1991 Soviet leader Mikhail Gorbachev announced the dismantling of the Union of Soviet Socialist Republics (USSR).

With the fragmentation of the former Soviet Union and the fall of communism in Europe, the Cold War ended. Its impact, however, is still felt today.

1 The Origins of the Cold War

Although many historians refer to World War II (1939–1945) as the beginning of the Cold War, tensions between Russia and the United States began long before that. Russia's turn to communism in 1917 was the beginning of an ideological rivalry between Russia and the United States that escalated throughout most of the century. The ideological contrasts would foster misunderstanding, mistrust, and mutual antagonism.

UNREST IN RUSSIA

At the turn of the twentieth century, Russia was a vast, militaristic country ruled by a czar, an all-powerful monarch. For centuries, Russia's class structure included a wealthy, land-owning upper class and an increasingly destitute peasant class tied to the land. The middle class, traditionally nearly nonexistent, had begun to grow in the 1880s and 1890s following rapid industrialization. Workers, however, were poorly paid; most labored in severely overcrowded conditions and few had any education.

The condition of the serfs, or peasants, was even worse. Even after uprisings forced the czar to implement land reforms, the majority were tied to communes, or group farming operations, which tended to perpetuate traditional and backward agricultural production and the feudal system. Peasants lacked money, education, and initiative to update their farming methods, and most found that they simply could not support themselves on the land. Some found temporary employment in nearby cities, others exhausted themselves toiling on the land. But no matter how hard they tried to alleviate their poverty, most of the peasants had limited success in improving their conditions.

By the early 1900s, Russia's dissatisfied industrial workers gave voice to the concerns of the Russian peasant class, sparking a radical opposition that grew increasingly critical of the current regime. Worker strikes, student protests, and peasant unrest spread. When workers marched on the czar's Winter Palace in a peaceful protest in 1905, police fired on the crowd, killing over 130 people. This massacre, known as "Bloody Sunday," became a rallying point in calls for revolution.

To quell the growing unrest, several months after Bloody Sunday the czar set up an elected and consultative body, called the Duma, Russia's first political

A Russian peasant family poses for a photograph in the early 1900s. It was at this time that peasants began to rise up against the government to call for a better quality of life.

body with true legislative functions. The Duma transformed Russia's governing structure into a constitutional monarchy. This gave the common people a say in politics for the first time in Russian history.

By 1917, however, economic conditions had not improved. Russia was exhausted by its participation in World War I. The country had suffered devastating human losses, inflation skyrocketed, and food and fuel were scarce. Angered by new bread rations in March, peasants and workers again rose in protest. This time strikes and mass demonstrations spread quickly, forcing czar Nicholas II to give up the throne.

Russia's parliament installed a provisional government that promoted liberty and democracy. Western nations praised the new government and its support for political freedom.

REVOLUTION

The new provisional government, however, failed to address the discontent among the peasants and workers. It continued Russia's participation in the war, despite mass calls for a negotiated peace. And although the government advocated land

Vladimir Lenin speaks to a crowd in Moscow in 1918, a year after he led the Bolshevik Revolution.

redistribution to the peasants, it did nothing to accomplish that goal. The government also failed to halt inflation, and Russia's economy continued its downward spiral. According to historian Nicholas V. Riasanovksy, the government "refused to recognize the catastrophic condition of the country and misjudged the mood of the people."[1] In addition, the intellectuals running the provisional government had few ties to the workers and peasants. In short, the government, like the czarist regime that had preceded it, was terribly out of touch with the needs of the masses. As a result, the provisional government lasted only a few months.

In October 1917 the Bolsheviks, a revolutionary group led by Vladimir Lenin, began a second Russian Revolution. Drawing on the writings of German philosopher Karl Marx, Lenin and his followers advocated a communist/socialist system that promoted equality and the elimination of social classes. Lenin called for the peasants and workers (called the proletariat) to rise up in protest of the current social and political structure and promised to end human exploitation and misery. The Bolsheviks seized power on November 7, when Bolshevik-led soldiers, sailors, and workers stormed the Winter Palace and arrested members of the provisional government. For Russia's poverty-stricken peasants and workers, who for so long had labored under extreme conditions for very little benefit, communism represented great hope for change.

The Marxist-Leninists predicted that socialist revolutions would ultimately spread throughout the world, overtaking capitalism and other forms of government. Lenin stated, "We have now learned to make a concerted effort. The revolution that has just been accomplished is evidence of this. We possess the strength of mass organization, which will overcome everything and lead the proletariat to the world revolution. . . . Long live the world socialist revolution."[2]

SEEDS OF THE CONFLICT

The United States was apprehensive about Russia's new politics. America's distrust of communism was rooted in its belief in the ideals of democracy and capitalism. The United States was established with a political system based on free elections, an economy based on a free market, and a social structure in which individuals expected to live with minimal governmental oversight. In the United States, citizens had made their own decisions about such things as what job to pursue or where to live. Through democratic elections, they chose their own leaders. Capitalist market forces of supply and demand determined what foods and other goods were available for purchase and at what price. Industries, for the most part, were owned by individuals or private corporations, rather than the government.

Bolshevik soldiers march through the streets of Moscow in protest of Russia's czarist government.

The ideology of communism contrasted sharply with the ideals the United States espoused. Under communism, the needs of the society as a whole were seen as more important than the needs of the individual. The state would temporarily control the means of production and hold political power until it was passed into the people's hands. Political leaders were not chosen through an election process, and thus citizens had little voice in who would lead them. And whereas under the czar only a small wealthy group of people owned Russia's land and industries, under communism, land and property were, in theory, owned by everyone.

The United States was both frustrated by the failure of democracy in Russia and

LENIN

Born Vladimir Ilyich Ulyanov, Lenin was the leader of the Bolshevik Revolution of 1917 and the founder of the Russian Communist Party. He was born in 1870 in Simbirsk (now Ulyanovsk), Russia, a small town on the Volga River. His father, a teacher and elementary education director, taught him strong values for bettering the life of fellow Russians. Lenin was a talented student in secondary school and while studying law at the University of Kazan.

At the age of nineteen, Lenin began to focus on the works of German philosopher Karl Marx. He believed that Marx's theory held the key to Russia's future, and that Russia could move from feudalism to communism without, as Marx theorized, moving through capitalism. Lenin developed his ideas, which came to be known as Marxist-Leninism, in a number of pamphlets and books.

A committed revolutionary, Lenin was imprisoned in 1896 and then exiled for three years in Siberia. After the ousting of the Russian czar during the February Revolution of 1917, Lenin spearheaded a group of revolutionaries, called Bolsheviks, to take control and form a new government based on the tenets of communism. Lenin created the Union of Soviet Socialist Republics (USSR) and led the country until his death in 1924.

He was a devoted communist, and in contrast to Stalin's later reliance on terror and the secret police, Lenin's leadership was based on his personality and ideological convictions. The cult of Lenin took on gigantic proportions in Soviet life; Lenin's writings and ideas were infused throughout Soviet propaganda and statues of him stood in the main squares of nearly every Soviet town.

Winston Churchill supported the decision to send European troops to stop the Red Army.

alarmed by Lenin's proclamations that socialism would spread throughout the world. Lenin declared, "As long as capitalism and socialism exist, we cannot live in peace; in the end one or the other will triumph."[3] If he was successful in Russia, would Europe be Lenin's next target? Would America itself one day be threatened?

THE UNITED STATES INTERVENES

Protecting freedom and democracy had become an important issue in American politics. In fact, the country had entered World War I with the aim of protecting democracy in Europe. When Germany and the Austro-Hungarian empire threatened to expand throughout Europe, the United States initially tried to remain neutral. After three years of conflict, however, the United States, guided by President Woodrow Wilson, finally came to the aid of Britain, France, and Russia in opposition to the Central Powers. In a speech given before Congress to gain its support for America's involvement, Wilson said that the country was ready to "fight thus for the ultimate peace of the world and for the liberation of its peoples, the German peoples included: for the rights of nations great and small and the privilege of men everywhere to choose their way of life and of obedience. The world must be made safe for democracy."[4]

America now took an active role in bringing its own ideals of democracy and self-determination to other parts of the world. As Bolshevism, or Russian communism, gained strength in Russia, the United States and other Western countries saw Russia as another arena where democracy was threatened.

The political upheaval in Russia at the close of World War I galvanized Western nations to subvert communism there. While the Bolsheviks worked to spread their ideas and consolidate their power, a number of groups emerged in opposition. Various groups located on the borders and advocating independence from Russia joined with counter-revolutionaries to form an army known as the White Army. In 1918, a bitter civil war erupted between the (Bolshevik) Reds and the Whites. Soon several western European countries sent troops into Russia to stop the Red Army, believing, as future British prime minister Winston Churchill admitted in 1919, it was necessary "to throttle the infant

A crowd gathers in front of the Winter Palace in Petrograd to hear Vladimir Lenin speak.

Bolshevism in its cradle."[5] Under the direction of President Wilson, the United States joined this movement, sending fifteen thousand American troops to Russian Siberia, participating in an economic blockade, and furnishing arms to anti-Bolshevik forces.

Despite the intervention, however, the Red Army was victorious. Lenin and his followers established communism throughout the former czarist empire in all regions except the European front. In 1922 Lenin announced a federation of republics called the Union of Soviet Socialist Republics (referred to as the USSR or the Soviet Union) that included vast territory in Russia, Ukraine, Belarus, and the Caucasus. Territory in Finland and Romania, and the

Baltic countries of Estonia, Latvia, and Lithuania were added in 1940.

FORGING COOPERATION AGAINST A COMMON ENEMY

The American interference on Russian soil in 1918 served only to embitter relations between the United States and the USSR. America's distrust of the Soviet Union continued in the years leading up to World War II, as the United States strongly objected to the brutal policies established by Lenin's successor, the totalitarian dictator Joseph Stalin. Stalin worked swiftly to transform the country from an agricultural economy to an advanced industrial nation, but he did so through unwise central planning and harsh austerity measures. While building new cities, workers often suffered from lack of food, shelter, and clothing. During Stalin's collectivization campaign in the 1920s and 1930s, the government seized privately owned farms and turned the property over to group, or collective, ownership. Peasants who opposed or resisted the measures were deported or killed. A terrible famine, brought about by both droughts and the collectivization process, followed, causing the deaths of millions of people. Within the government, the suspicious Stalin used even harsher measures. He ordered the executions of fellow Communist Party members during random purges in an attempt to eliminate any possible rivals.

By 1937 Stalin's terror extended to all parts of Soviet life. Ordinary workers and farmers feared being labeled an enemy of the Communist Party, which meant the loss of their jobs, their friends, and often their lives. Western observers watched in horror as Stalin randomly imprisoned, exiled, or killed all kinds of prominent Soviet citizens including politicians, artists, doctors, and scientists. It became increasingly clear to the United States and other nations that Stalin was a ruthless dictator who would stop at nothing to solidify his power.

By the early 1930s, however, the attention of Western nations was focused on another ruthless dictator, German Nazi

Joseph Stalin eliminated Soviet citizens who he deemed to be enemies of the Communist Party.

Adolf Hitler, who had risen to power in Germany and whose territorial ambitions threatened the rest of Europe. In 1938 Hitler sent soldiers to Austria to annex that nation to Germany.

Western nations thought they could avoid war by satisfying some of Hitler's demands for territory. To this end, British and French representatives traveled to Munich in 1938, where they signed an agreement with Germany allowing it to take parts of the country of Czechoslovakia. Stalin, who had been poised to assist Czechoslovakia, was outraged, as he had not even been invited to the Munich talks. Now, rather than seeking to join with the British and others to foil Hitler, Stalin decided to cooperate with Hitler in an effort to protect the Soviet border. In 1939 Stalin and Hitler signed a secret pact in which each of their countries promised that it would never attack the other. The agree-

---

STALIN

Historian Nicholas V. Riasanovsky explains in A History of Russia *that despite Joseph Stalin's modest beginnings and his study of Marxism, he used his position as the leader of the Communist Party to abandon Lenin's message and became one of the most totalitarian and feared dictators of all time:*

"Stalin participated in the historic events of 1917, and after the October Revolution he became the first commissar for national minorities. . . . But Stalin's real bid for power began in 1922 with his appointment as general secretary of the Party, a position that gave him broad authority in matters of personnel.

The long-time official Soviet view of Stalin as Lenin's anointed successor distorts reality, for in fact, the ailing Bolshevik leader came to resent the general secretary's rigidity and rudeness and in his so-called testament warned the Party leadership against Stalin. But Stalin's rivals failed to heed Lenin's late forebodings, and, before too long, Stalin's Party machine rolled over all opponents. The complete personal dictatorship which began in 1928 was to last until the dictator's death in 1953. . . .

In addition to fighting real battles and struggles against actual opponents, Stalin lived in the paranoiac world of constant threat and wholesale conspiracy. Fact and fantasy were blended together, making the detection of the dictator's motives extremely difficult. . . . Paranoiac tendencies joined with Marxism in transforming the Russian scene."

Adolf Hitler salutes Nazi troops in Nuremberg. Hitler and Stalin secretly agreed that neither of their countries would attack the other.

ment included plans to divide eastern Europe and to dismantle and divide Poland. Hitler's invasion of Poland in September 1939 began World War II, pitting Germany and Fascist Italy against Great Britain and France.

Despite Hitler and Stalin's pact, Germany which already occupied France, the Netherlands, Belgium, and other parts of Europe, invaded the Soviet Union on June 22, 1941. By this time the Axis powers—primarily Germany, Japan, and Italy—had been at war with the Allies for nearly two years and were poised to invade Great Britain. Hitler's invasion of the Soviet Union provoked a betrayed Stalin to join

Japan attacks U.S. ships in Pearl Harbor. This event led to the United States' formal entrance into World War II.

the Allies. The United States formally entered the war with the Allies in December, when Japanese forces attacked the U.S. naval base in Pearl Harbor, Hawaii.

By the fall of 1941, the Nazis had swiftly won positions in Belorussia and Ukraine. German armies held the city of Leningrad (now St. Petersburg) under siege and were moving dangerously close (within fifteen miles of) to the capital city of Moscow.

Although defeat seemed imminent, Stalin moved quickly to reorganize and revamp the Red Army and launch a counterattack. The determination of the Soviets, coupled with a bitterly cold winter that caught the Nazis unprepared, allowed the Soviet military to save Moscow and to move into an offensive position. Soviet victories mounted, and by early 1943 the Red Army had forced the German retreat in Russia. The siege of

Leningrad was partly broken in 1943 and fully removed in January 1944. Soviet tanks now rolled toward Europe to take on and defeat German troops there.

Thus, from 1941 to 1945, despite their opposition to Stalin's domestic policies, now Prime Minister Winston Churchill and American President Franklin D. Roosevelt welcomed Stalin as a necessary partner in the struggle to defeat Nazi Germany. When facing the common threat of Nazi takeover, the Allied countries had been able to put their differences aside. As an Allied victory became imminent, however, the United States, England, and the Soviet Union began to discuss their aims for postwar Europe, and disagreements arose.

A FLAWED PEACE PROCESS: THE MEETING AT YALTA

In February 1945, Roosevelt, Churchill, and Stalin traveled to Yalta, the former summer retreat of the Russian czars, to discuss plans for the postwar peace and German war reparations. The leaders came to this sum-

Churchill, Roosevelt, and Stalin (seated left to right) meet in Yalta to negotiate plans for peace after World War II.

mit with differing, and incompatible, objectives. Stalin first and foremost wanted security. To protect the Soviet Union, Stalin demanded a wide buffer zone of friendly territory in eastern Europe. He felt that this control was needed to ensure that a foreign invader could never again penetrate the borders of the Soviet Union. Churchill, however, wanted to make sure that no single power would dominate Europe, which seemed to be what Stalin's demands were leading to. Roosevelt wanted to finalize plans for the creation of the United Nations, as he believed the United States could exercise its influence in European affairs through this organization. Both the United States and Britain also hoped to get Stalin's cooperation to help end the fighting in the Pacific.

Stalin's bargaining position was strong. Without the help of the Soviet army, the Allies might not have been able to defeat Hitler. According to Soviet statistics, the Red Army had defeated a total of 506 German divisions and was responsible for 10 million of the 13.6 million German casualties. Yet victory had come at a huge cost to the Soviets. The war had inflicted significant material damage in Russia, Ukraine, and Belarus. Fighting on Soviet territory had destroyed about thirty-two thousand factories and about sixty-five thousand kilometers of railway track. Furthermore, the Soviets suffered staggering human casualties, with more than 25 million Soviets killed during World War II. Because of the destruction done to the Soviet Union and the obvious need to secure Soviet borders, Stalin demanded monetary and territorial compensation.

The issue of Poland dominated the discussions at Yalta. The Soviets were sponsoring the procommunist Polish Liberation Army while Western governments had put their support behind a democratic-leaning government in exile in London. Stalin repeatedly stressed the need for a communist-friendly government in Warsaw: "Throughout history Poland has been a corridor through which the enemy has passed into Russia. Twice, in the last 30 years our enemies, the Germans, have passed through this corridor. . . . Poland is not only a question of honor but also of life and death for the Soviet Union."[6] Stalin also wanted new boundaries that would give Russia part of Poland in the east, and allot Poland part of Germany in the west.

COMPROMISES AND DISPUTES

Churchill was determined to reinstate the Polish government that was in exile in England. He protested vehemently the proposed plan for Poland. Eventually, Roosevelt was able to broker a compromise: Russia would get the boundary to the east and the issue of the boundary to the west would be postponed. As for Poland's government, it was agreed that a broad coalition would be installed that would include members of the group in exile. Free elections would be held in Poland in the future. Stalin also signed the Declaration on Liberated Europe that pledged to foster the conditions for future democratic elections in Europe. Although these agreements were somewhat vague, it was the best the leaders could agree upon.

Alexis de Tocqueville's Vision

As early as the 1830s, French aristocrat and political philosopher Alexis de Tocqueville, author of Democracy in America, *predicted the rise of America and Russia and the ideological struggle that would break out between them. Over a hundred years before it became a reality, his vision is striking in its ability to predict that one day the differing outlooks could split the world into two camps:*

"There are on earth today two great people, who from different points of departure, seem to be advancing toward the same end. They are the Russians and the Anglo-Americans. Both have grown great in obscurity; and while the attention of mankind was occupied elsewhere they have suddenly taken their places in the first rank among the nations, and the world had learned, almost at the same time, both of their birth and of their greatness.

All other peoples appear to have attained approximately their natural limits, and have nothing left but to preserve their positions; but these two are growing; all the others have stopped or continue only by endless effort; they alone advance easily and rapidly in a career of which the limit cannot yet be seen. . . .

The one has liberty as the chief way of doing things; the other servitude. Their points of departure are different. Their paths are divergent; nevertheless each seems summoned by a secret design of providence to hold in his hands, some day, the destinies of half the world."

At Yalta, Stalin agreed to join in the fight against Japan as quickly as two or three months after the final defeat of Hitler. In addition, the Soviet Union agreed to join the United Nations. The leaders resolved that Germany would be partitioned into four occupation zones, one each for the United States, the Soviet Union, Britain, and France. Stalin insisted that he was entitled to huge reparations from Germany. Although England and the United States were opposed to reparations, they eventually agreed to the amount of $20 billion worth of goods and equipment, one-half of which would go to the Soviet Union. Further decisions on reparations would take place after the war's end.

Despite the agreements reached at Yalta, the summit revealed weaknesses in the grand alliance. Several disputes had been narrowly avoided, and Roosevelt had found Stalin increasingly difficult to negotiate with. Because the war had left only two major countries, the United States and the Soviet Union, with sufficient power and influence to rebuild and redefine the postwar world, continuing cooperation would be needed in peacetime.

Clearly, compromise between the two countries would be difficult in part because each country saw itself in the role of leader of the world. The Soviet Union had emerged from the fighting in Europe as a major military power. World War II had forced Stalin to develop an awesome military prowess, and now his country felt it was ready and entitled to shape politics, especially in Eastern Europe. The United States had also emerged from the war in a position of great power and saw itself as the country to lead the world.

The United States had created a powerful war economy. Before the war many people could not find employment due to the Great Depression, but during the war there were lots of jobs manufacturing arms, machinery, and other goods. The United States economy more than doubled from 1939 to 1945, and its gross national product (GNP) increased from $90 billion to $212 billion. As World War II came to an end, the United States wanted to continue exporting goods to Europe and elsewhere to maintain its economic boom. Recognizing the strong leadership role of the United States, many war-torn countries looked to America for financial assistance as they attempted to rebuild their economies.

It is difficult to say whether the Soviet Union and the United States were on a collision course that could not be avoided. But as each country set about the task of leading the postwar world, underlying tensions intensified. The death of Roosevelt shortly after Yalta may have worsened matters. America's new president, Harry S. Truman, seemed less willing to negotiate with Stalin. Whereas Roosevelt had been patient and diplomatic in dealing with the Soviets, Truman proved brazen and direct. Churchill noted that Truman "takes no notice of middle ground, he just plants his foot firmly on it."[7] Now it was up to Truman to smooth tensions with Stalin and to forge collaboration between the United States and the USSR. Unfortunately, difficult personalities, opposing ideologies, and historical events would make simple cooperation between the two superpowers increasingly problematic.

2 Cold War Tensions Divide Europe

The events of the immediate postwar years, and the policies adopted in the United States and in the Soviet Union in reaction to these events, divided Europe. Leaders in both countries interpreted the actions of the other as aggressive. The clash between capitalism and communism, and between the United States and the USSR, split Europe into two competing parts: This split both defined and intensified the Cold War.

THE MEETINGS AT POTSDAM

When Truman took over the presidency, it became clear that Roosevelt had kept his vice president poorly informed on foreign policy. Truman came to a quick conclusion that the USSR was simply a bully in Europe and should be forced to change its ways. The new U.S. president was especially dismayed by Moscow's actions in Poland. Conservative Poles exiled in London had not been included in the Polish government and elections had not yet been held, in violation of the agreements reached at Yalta.

Less than two weeks after taking office, Truman called Soviet foreign minister Vy-

acheslav Molotov to the White House. Truman scolded Molotov for violating the Yalta accords and dictated that the Soviets should honor their agreements. Molotov stormed out of the room. Truman was apparently pleased with his tough policy, boasting later, "I gave it to him straight one-two to the jaw. I let him have it straight."[8] Molotov, however, was furious, stating, "I have never been talked to like that in my life."[9] This hard-hitting approach on both sides would soon become typical in Cold War relations. The era of negotiation and cooperation forged at Yalta was coming to an end.

When Truman, Churchill, and Stalin met in Potsdam, Germany, in July 1945, relations continued to decline. From the start, the three leaders could not agree on anything. Truman proposed that they discuss the reorganization of the governments of Romania and Bulgaria and free elections there. Stalin preferred to discuss issues such as reparations from Germany, moving Poland's western frontier, and eliminating Poland's government in exile. Though Churchill attended the first session, he was replaced as prime minister by Clement Attlee, who had to step in for the British. Historian Stephen E. Ambrose

Representatives of the United States, the U.S.S.R., and Great Britain attend the first formal meeting of the Potsdam Conference.

explains, "Arguments went on and on, with some minor agreements reached, but nothing important could be settled. . . . Snipping and jabbing were the hallmarks of Potsdam."[10]

The Allied leaders did agree on some policies for governing Germany. A control council, made up of the military commanders of the country's four zones was empowered to dismantle and demilitarize the former Nazi regime. In the matter of reparations, the British suggested that each occupying nation take reparations from its own zone. This agreement was a concession by the Soviets, as it meant that they would have to relinquish any claims on the mining-rich areas of the Ruhr Valley. The Soviets yielded on the issue of the Ruhr Valley in exchange for final approval of a new Polish boundary as discussed in depth at Yalta

While he was at the Potsdam meetings, Truman learned that American scientists had successfully tested the world's first atomic bomb. The new uranium bomb boasted far greater firepower than conventional bombs and could explode with a blast equal to thousands of tons of TNT. Feeling, therefore, that he no longer needed Stalin's help in defeating Japan, Truman became even less diplomatic. According to Molotov:

> Truman decided to surprise us at Potsdam. . . . He took Stalin and me aside and—looking secretive—informed us they had a secret weapon of a wholly new type, an extraordinary weapon. . . . It's difficult to say what he was thinking, but it seemed to me he wanted to throw us into consternation. Stalin, however, reacted to this quite calmly and Truman decided he hadn't understood. The words atomic bomb hadn't been spoken, but we immediately guessed what he meant.[11]

THE MANHATTAN PROJECT

The Manhattan Project was a top secret collaboration among the United States, Britain, and Canada to develop the world's first atomic bomb. American physicist J. Robert Oppenheimer directed the project and set up a laboratory in Los Alamos, New Mexico, where the bomb was designed and built. Fearing that the Nazis were developing the bomb as well, the scientists sped to successfully split the atom in the process called fission. About thirty-seven research sites and 120,000 people contributed to the project that cost Washington over $2 billion. Although the Manhattan Project was highly classified, many Soviet spies were able to infiltrate it, including Klaus Fuchs, a communist German physicist who worked directly in Los Alamos. These spies helped the Soviet Union to produce its own atomic bomb by 1949. Nonetheless, the Manhattan Project was successful. On July 16, 1945, in the deserts of New Mexico, the first atom bomb was tested under the code name Trinity. According to Isaacs and Downing in *Cold War: An Illustrated History 1945–1991*, one of the scientists present at the test wrote the following description of the test explosion of the atomic bomb:

"Suddenly, there was an enormous flash of light, the brightest light I have ever seen or that I think anyone has even seen. . . . Finally it was over, diminishing, and we looked toward the place where the bomb had been; there was an enormous ball of fire which grew and grew, and it rolled as it grew. . . . A new thing had just been born; a new control. A new understanding of man, which man had acquired over nature."

THE UNITED STATES DROPS THE ATOMIC BOMB

Truman returned from Potsdam with a superior attitude. The United States was the only country in the world to possess the atomic bomb. The weapon, together with the economic strength of the United States, gave the president and his advisers confidence in American superiority, especially with regard to the Soviet Union. The United States believed it could stop the Soviets from spreading communism worldwide simply by threatening to use the bomb. Historian Stephen E. Ambrose writes, "From Potsdam on, the bomb was the constant factor in the American approach to the Soviet Union."[12]

The United States wasted no time showing the Soviets and the world that it had the bomb and was not afraid to use it. On August 6, 1945, the United States detonated the first atom bomb over Hiroshima, Japan. The bomb exploded at eighteen hundred feet with a force equivalent to thirteen thousand tons of TNT, and the blast destroyed the city within minutes. As many as one hundred thousand civilians were killed instantly.

Despite the fact that Stalin declared war on Japan two days later, the United States detonated a second atomic bomb over Na-

Wreckage and debris litter the ground at Nagasaki, Japan. Nagasaki was the second city to be obliterated by an atomic bomb at the end of World War II.

gasaki, Japan, on August 9. Like Hiroshima, Nagasaki suffered dreadful casualties and significant damage. The Japanese surrendered the following day. The mighty American military had brought the fighting in the Pacific to an end. America celebrated the bomb as a military and scientific breakthrough. At war's end, many Americans believed that the United States was now the most powerful nation on earth.

In the Soviet Union the existence of the bomb only served to reinforce the Soviet position to avoid military conflict with the West. According to Stalin's adviser Maxim Litvinov in 1944, the Soviets still sought "some kind of cooperation in order to have at least a few decades of peace." Even so, the Soviets still intended to have a say in defining the postwar world. They continued to argue that their borders must be secured against foreign invaders. The United States, they reasoned, was located far from the shores of Europe and should be more concerned with events taking place in neighboring countries such as those in Latin America. Litvinov continued, "One would imagine that the United States would be most responsible for the security of the countries on the American continent, and a certain part of the Pacific and Atlantic oceans."[13]

Thus the Soviets went about securing their buffer zone in Eastern Europe. By the end of 1945, pro-Soviet governments were set up in Romania and Bulgaria and were already in effect in Poland. The United States viewed the Soviet expansion with alarm. Truman and his advisers began to worry that Stalin was making plans to spread communism worldwide.

THE U.S. POLICY OF CONTAINMENT: THE TRUMAN DOCTRINE AND THE MARSHALL PLAN

A speech by Stalin in February 1946 compounded these fears. Stalin indicated that capitalism threatened the world, saying, "The development of world capitalism, proceeds not in the path of smooth and even progress but through crisis and the catastrophes of war."[14] Stalin also alluded to the fact that the great powers should settle their disputes by acknowledging "spheres of influence," meaning that countries would be allowed some political, military, or economic influence over other nations that were on its borders or of some other strategic importance.

This point, however, went unnoticed by American officials who now worried that Stalin wanted war. According to recent historical accounts, Stalin probably did not intend to threaten war with the West. Historians Jeremy Isaacs and Taylor Downing explain that "although in his speeches he paid lip service to the old Marxist ideal of world revolution, . . . there is no hard evidence that Stalin ever realistically thought about invading the West. Despite the strength of the Red Army, Stalin knew that technologically he was still weaker than his opponents. And in the immediate postwar years, America had the atom bomb and the Soviet Union did not."[15]

Nonetheless, American policy makers were highly troubled by the speech. Deciding that it was time to understand Stalin's aims and motives in more depth, the State Department sent a request for further information to the U.S. embassy in

Winston Churchill (left) and Harry S. Truman (right) raise their arms in triumph after Churchill delivered his "Iron Curtain" speech.

Moscow. The task of answering was assigned to George Kennan, an analyst and scholar of Russia working at the embassy.

In what became known as the "Long Telegram," Kennan wrote that Stalin's policies were rooted in Russian history, a history that proved the country was isolated, paranoid, and cruel. Kennan predicted an inevitable long-term struggle between communism and democracy. He wrote that the Soviet leaders "found justification for their instinctive fear of the outside world, for the dictatorship without which they did not know how to rule, for cruelties they did not dare not to inflict."[16] He stressed that the Soviet Union could only be dealt with through force.

Many policy makers agreed with Kennan's assessment. Senator J. William Fulbright later recalled, "After World War Two, we were sold on the idea that Stalin was out to dominate the world."[17] The United States was now convinced that the Soviet Union was expansionist, powerful, and ruthless. This sentiment was cultivated further in a dramatic speech given by Churchill in Fulton, Missouri, on March 5, 1946. With Truman in attendance, the former British prime minister said of Europe, "From Stettin in the Baltic, to Trieste in the Adriatic, an iron curtain has descended across the continent."[18] The statement seemed to confirm what both sides feared, that the world was now divided between East and West.

In the Soviet Union, the speech was enough to convince Stalin that the West was antagonistic and aggressive and that the United States and Great Britain were conspiring against him. He denounced Churchill's speech as a call to war. *Pravda*, the Communist Party newspaper, labeled

EXCERPTS FROM CHURCHILL'S IRON CURTAIN SPEECH

Speaking at Westminster College in Fulton, Missouri, on March 5, 1946, Winston Churchill gave a powerful and memorable speech in which he warned of Soviet expansionism. In the speech, archived at the CNN Cold War website, Churchill coined the phrase "iron curtain" to explain the line that now divided the world into two incompatible political camps.

From Stettin in the Baltic to Trieste in the Adriatic, an iron curtain has descended across the Continent. Behind that line lie all the capitals of the ancient states of Central and Eastern Europe. Warsaw, Berlin, Prague, Vienna, Budapest, Belgrade, Bucharest and Sofia, all these famous cities and the populations around them lie in what I must call the Soviet sphere, and all are subject in one form or another, not only to Soviet influence but to a very high and, in many cases, increasing measure of control from Moscow. . . . The communist parties, which were very small in all these eastern states of Europe, have been raised to pre-eminence and power far beyond their numbers and are seeking everywhere to obtain totalitarian control. Police governments are prevailing in nearly every case, and so far, except in Czechoslovakia, there is no true democracy.

I do not believe that Soviet Russia desires war. What they desire is the fruits of war and the indefinite expansion of their power and doctrines. But what we have to consider here today while time remains is the permanent prevention of war and the establishment of conditions of freedom and democracy as rapidly as possible in all countries. Our difficulties and dangers will not be removed by closing our eyes to them. They will not be removed by mere waiting to see what happens; nor will they be removed by a policy of appeasement. What is needed is a settlement, and the longer this is delayed, the more difficult it will be and the greater our dangers will become.

. . . From what I have seen of our Russian friends and Allies during the war, I am convinced that there is nothing they admire so much as strength, and there is nothing for which they have less respect than for weakness, especially military weakness. . . . If the Western democracies stand together in strict adherence to the principles of the United Nations Charter, their influence for furthering those principles will be immense and no one is likely to molest them. If however they become divided or falter in their duty and if these all-important years are allowed to slip away then indeed catastrophe may overwhelm us all.

Churchill a warmonger and a racist. Only a year after the meetings at Yalta, the wartime alliance had disintegrated completely.

Tensions continued to escalate with President Truman's address to Congress on March 12, 1947. The president asked for $400 million in aid for Greece and Turkey. Britain had recently withdrawn economic aid to the area, and the United States feared the region might now fall to communism. In alarmist language, Truman made clear

George C. Marshall created a plan to help Europe recover from its bad economic downturn after World War II.

that any threat to peace should be seen as a threat to the security of the United States. His speech was the first official voicing of a policy that came to be called the Truman Doctrine. The United States was committed to opposing the spread of communism worldwide and would intervene, by force if necessary, in any threatened area. Truman stated, "It must be the policy of the U.S. to support free peoples who are resisting attempted subjugation by armed minorities or by outside pressures."[19]

The president warned that if Greece and Turkey fell to communism, other countries in Western Europe, Africa, and the Middle East would also one day be threatened. Truman also described two distinct ways of life, one rooted in freedom and independence and the other in totalitarianism. Having alluded to the ideological struggle between these two rivals, Truman's speech was successful. Congress approved the financial package, and containment policy was swiftly legitimized in the United States.

The rift between East and West was deepened when Secretary of State George C. Marshall outlined his plan for Europe's economic recovery. In a speech on June 5, 1947, Marshall announced that the U.S. government would finance a European recovery program. He spoke of the grave economic circumstances for European countries that had yet to recover from the war, circumstances that had been worsened by an especially cold winter that had depleted supplies of coal and other commodities. Marshall stated, "It is logical that the United States should do whatever it is able to do to assist in the return of normal economic health in the world, without which there can be no political stability and no assured peace."[20] The so-called Marshall Plan offered financial aid to European governments but insisted that the money must be used to buy American products. In this way, the aid would not only rebuild Europe but also stimulate the American economy.

Because Marshall's invitation was broad, it was unclear to the Soviets whether they too could apply for the aid. Marshall did not specify which countries were eligible, saying only, "Our policy is directed not against any country or doctrine, but against hunger, poverty, desperation, and chaos. Its purpose should be the revival of the working economy in the world so as to permit the emergence of political and social conditions in which free institutions can exist."[21] Although Molotov pushed for the Soviets to participate, Stalin believed that the plan was aimed solely at Europe. He said, "This is a ploy by Truman. . . . They don't want to help us. What they want is to infiltrate European countries."[22]

The plan was indeed political as well as economic. The Truman administration hoped to prevent the spread of communism by making Europe's governments more stable and secure. Stalin, understanding this, read the policy as aggressive and assumed that the United States was scheming to bring Eastern Europe under Western control. Thus, when invitations to the Marshall Plan Paris conference went out to all Western European states as well as to Romania, Bulgaria, Hungary, Albania, Finland, Yugoslavia, Poland, and Czechoslovakia, the Soviet Union instructed its satellite countries to refuse the offer.

When the Czechs planned to travel to Paris anyway, Stalin immediately called their representatives to Moscow. He warned them that their participation would be seen as an attempt to undermine and betray the Soviet Union. Fearful of the consequences of disobeying the Soviet leader, the Czechoslovak delegation quickly canceled their plans. Czech foreign minister Jan Masaryk recalled, "I went to Moscow as the foreign minister of an independent sovereign state; I returned a Soviet slave."[23]

In essence the Marshall Plan forced the line between East and West. No longer could European nations remain indecisive or neutral. Each country, in effect, was forced to choose allegiance to either the Western alliance or the Soviet bloc. As the Western European delegates met in Paris to discuss their applications for U.S. aid, Communist Party leaders convened in the village of Szlianka Poremba in Poland. They created a new socialist alliance, Cominform, aimed to fuse and strengthen the socialist countries in Eastern Europe and to consolidate Soviet control over its satellite countries.

THE BERLIN BLOCKADE, NATO, AND THE SOVIET BOMB

With most of Europe divided into two distinct camps, the question of Germany's future became more pressing. The United States believed that the economic recovery

COMMUNISTS IN YUGOSLAVIA

Yugoslavia, led by Josip Broz Tito, was the sole country in Eastern Europe that arrived at communism without the assistance of the Soviet Union. Tito's independence caused significant tension between Yugoslavia and the USSR, as explained by Jeremy Isaacs and Taylor Downing in Cold War, An Illustrated History, 1945–1991.

"The Communist Party in Yugoslavia came to power at the end of the Second World War without Soviet help, unlike what happened in other East European states. Marshal Josip Broz Tito, the charismatic partisan leader, took power on his own initiative, and through sheer force of character held together the fragile union of the Yugoslav provinces, Montenegro, Serbia, Slovenia, Croatia, Macedonia, and the Bosnia-Herzegovina. Tito did all he could to exhibit his loyalty to the socialist cause, but there was tension in his relationship with Moscow from the start. Tito was secure at home, internationally renowned, and too independent-minded to suit Stalin.

The Kremlin dictator expected nothing less than total obedience from his satellites. But for Tito, Yugoslavia had earned the right to determine its own destiny. In foreign affairs, Belgrade insisted on following its own line and did not seek advice or approval from Moscow.... Through the early months of 1948, as the split grew worse, Moscow accused Belgrade of misbehaviors and of ideological deviation from the true socialist cause. Every denial by the Yugoslavs further enraged the Kremlin. Tito refused to give way, saying in March, 'We are not pawns on a chessboard.'

Then, on 28 June, only four days after launching the blockade against Berlin, Moscow expelled Yugoslavia from Cominform and called on other Communist parties to isolate Tito. An economic blockade was organized against Yugoslavia that caused great hardship, but Belgrade stood firm. Rejected by the East, Tito over the next twelve months turned slowly . . . towards the West. Following a disastrous harvest in 1949, a trade agreement was signed with the United Sates by which Yugoslavia opened its borders. Although not technically a member of the Plan, Yugoslavia went on to receive about $150 million in aid from the United Sates. Throughout the Cold War, Yugoslavia would remain the only independent Communist state in Europe."

of Germany was needed to boost economies throughout Europe. The British, French, and Americans had begun to consolidate their zones into one capitalist state and discussed the creation of a separate West German state, with an independent government friendly to the West. This plan threatened the Soviets, who had been pushing for negotiations to discuss a united Germany that, it hoped, might fall under the influence of the Eastern bloc.

Meanwhile, the former German capital of Berlin, which was also divided into four zones, was located deep within Soviet-controlled German territory. Using this fact to their advantage, in June 1948, the Soviets refused to allow Western countries access to their zones in Berlin. The Soviets halted all overland and river traffic to Berlin in an effort to force the Western nations out of the city. Rather than negotiate with the Soviets, Truman ordered a massive airlift of supplies, including coal, eggs, dried milk, medicines, and blankets, to the city. The Berlin airlift lasted for eleven months and delivered supplies to 2.5 million Germans. Unwilling to push the crisis further, in May 1949 the Soviets lifted the blockade.

The Berlin blockade was clearly an attempt to push the Western powers out of Germany, thereby thwarting the creation

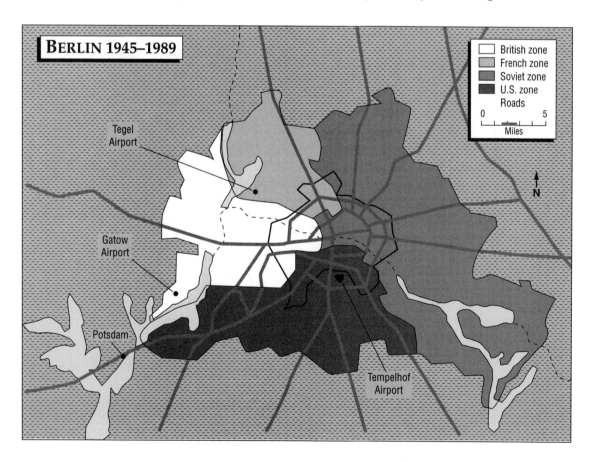

of a West German state. Stalin thought the blockade would bully Western leaders into agreeing to discuss German reunification. Instead, while the United States was operating daily flights of supplies to Berlin, a new constitution was being drafted. After the blockade was lifted, the Federal Republic of Germany, known as West Germany, was created. Stalin's aim to thwart the division of Germany was unsuccessful. In retaliation, the Soviets founded the German Democratic Republic, or East Germany, and proclaimed East Berlin its capital.

Also during the Berlin blockade, the United States, Britain, France, Canada, and eight other nations established the North Atlantic Treaty Organization, or NATO. NATO's member nations agreed to participate in their collective security, meaning an attack on one nation would be seen as an attack against all, to be responded to accordingly. Truman administration officials claimed that NATO would make Europe politically cohesive and give countries the confidence to stand firm against communist pressures. As part of the commitment, American troops and nuclear weapons

People in Berlin wait for fruit provided by the United States to be distributed. President Truman ordered that food and supplies be airlifted to Germany.

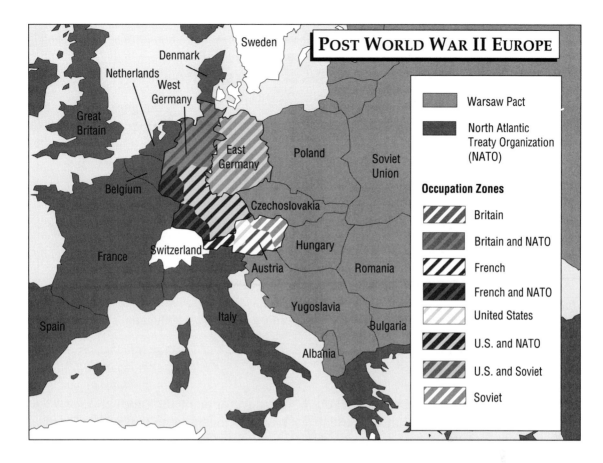

POST WORLD WAR II EUROPE

Legend:
- Warsaw Pact
- North Atlantic Treaty Organization (NATO)

Occupation Zones
- Britain
- Britain and NATO
- French
- French and NATO
- United States
- U.S. and NATO
- U.S. and Soviet
- Soviet

Map labels: Sweden, Denmark, Netherlands, West Germany, Great Britain, East Germany, Poland, Soviet Union, Belgium, Czechoslovakia, France, Switzerland, Hungary, Austria, Romania, Spain, Italy, Yugoslavia, Bulgaria, Albania

would be stationed in Western Europe. Although critics of NATO, such as Senator Robert A. Taft of Ohio, claimed that NATO would gravely endanger American soldiers and might provoke an arms race with the Soviets, the U.S. Senate ratified the treaty by a vote of 82 to 13. Within a few years, NATO would have fifteen members and would serve as the main military means to contain the Soviets in Europe.

NATO was important for a number of reasons. Initially it was a crushing disappointment for the Soviets. It was clear to the Soviet leadership that this military alliance, the first of its kind established during peacetime, was aimed aggressively against the Soviet Union. NATO also served to foster greater political, economic, and social ties among participating countries in Western Europe. It was a tangible and clear marker that Europe was now firmly divided between a capitalist West and a communist East. According to historian Michael Kort, "Its very existence was a major step in the institutionalization of the Cold War."[24]

To counter NATO, the Soviets established their own military alliance of East European countries in 1955, known as the Warsaw Pact. For more than thirty-five years, NATO and Warsaw Pact troops faced off in Europe.

U.S. GOVERNMENT REORGANIZES TO PREPARE FOR SOVIET THREAT

With containment and the Truman Doctrine, it became clear that American foreign policy was focused on preventing communist aggression by its rival, the Soviet Union. A number of new U.S. governmental agencies were created to further this goal, most of which still remain important in the conduct of U.S. foreign policy today. In July 1947, the passing of the National Security Act created the Department of Defense, the National Security Commission, and the Central Intelligence Agency (CIA), which was responsible for intelligence gathering and covert activities. These three agencies would be instrumental throughout the many years of Cold War conduct. In 1953, the U.S. government would add the United States Information Agency (USIA), whose priority mission was to "counter Soviet propaganda" and spread pro-American sentiment.

Shortly after the inception of NATO, the United States learned that the Soviet Union had successfully detonated an atomic bomb. The United States no longer had the monopoly on nuclear weapons. The discovery caused great worry among NATO countries; almost overnight, it seemed, the Western bloc had lost its clear advantage in world politics. The U.S. government reacted to this troubling development in the defensive manner that had become customary in the early days of the Cold War. While Moscow was advocating peaceful coexistence with the United States, Secretary of State Dean Acheson announced that there would be no appeasement of the Soviets. Assuring the world that the United States would remain on top, President Truman ordered the development and production of a "super" hydrogen bomb that would be more powerful than the weapons of the Soviets.

Thus began the era of misunderstanding, suspicion, and fear known as the Cold War. The world had been split into two competing blocs led by the Soviet Union and the United States. Each country believed in its political and social structure and felt threatened by the other. Both countries felt they were entitled to manipulate the affairs of other countries, with the aim of stopping the other aggressor. According to historian Mary Beth Norton, "Each sought leadership in reassembling the world order; each sought to build up its own sphere of influence; each was driven by an ideology and a sense of righteousness."[25]

3 The Cold War Spreads to Asia

With the divisions of the Cold War clearly marked in Europe, the Soviet-American rivalry quickly spread to other parts of the globe. Asia would prove to be the first battleground where the United States and the Soviet Union would compete to win influence and gain allies while each subverting the other.

POSTWAR RECONSTRUCTION OF JAPAN

Just as postwar Germany was demilitarized and postwar Europe rebuilt, the defeat of the Japanese empire called for attention in Asia. After the Allied victory, the two superpowers set about the reorganization of Asian territory formerly occupied by Japan. In what was meant to be a temporary solution, Korea was divided along the 38th parallel; Soviet forces would oversee the northern part of the country, and American forces would be stationed in the south. It was also decided that America would gain control over island groups in the Pacific, including the Marshalls, Marianas, and Carolines. As had been agreed at the Yalta Conference, Southern Sakhalin and the Kurile Islands,

obtained by the Soviets in the 1941 Nazi-Soviet pact, reverted to Russian control. Formosa, or Taiwan, was returned to China.

The Japanese reconstruction efforts revealed the first signs of tension between the superpowers in Asia. It was quickly apparent that the United States intended to dominate postwar activities in Japan. Led by General Douglas MacArthur, the Americans worked to destroy Japanese weapons and warships, while at the same time assisting in the drafting of Japan's new constitution. Britain and Russia, however, felt that, having contributed to the defeat of Japan, they were entitled to a voice in Japanese reconstruction. In response, Averell Harriman, the U.S. ambassador to Japan, simply replied that the Truman administration was "very firm on the matter of keeping the power in American hands."[26]

Refusing to recognize U.S. supremacy in Japan, the Soviet Union argued with the United States for several years about the specifics of a Japanese peace treaty. Nikita Khrushchev, who had served in the Red Army during World War II and would go on to become the Soviet leader from 1953 to 1964, later described the

General Douglas MacArthur (left) and President Truman assisted Japan in drafting a new constitution after World War II.

Soviets' role as "that of a poor relative at the wedding of a rich man. We were ignored."[27] No agreement could be reached.

The United States finally signed a treaty with Japan in 1951. Stalin, who was invited to join, refused to sign the treaty. The treaty ended the six-year postwar Allied occupation and restored sovereignty to Japan. The Americans were allowed to keep a military base in Okinawa. Although the separate treaty angered the Soviets, America had found a new ally in its former archrival Japan. George Kennan aptly called Japan, along with Germany, one of "our most important pawns on the chessboard of world politics."[28]

THE LOSS OF CHINA

Meanwhile, China had taken center stage in the Cold War rivalry in Asia. China's nationalist army and leader Chiang Kai-shek had been fighting Mao Zedong's communist forces for political control since 1927. The United States had been sending military aid to Chiang Kai-shek since 1946, while the Soviets were backing Mao.

Although Chiang's administration was corrupt, the Americans feared decreasing support would enable the communists to gain footing in Asia. Despite the American assistance, however, Chiang's internal support was faltering. He was increasingly

criticized for ignoring peasant demands for land redistribution and for tolerating an unfair tax system. American officials urged Chiang to weed out corruption, to reduce inflation, and to promote land reform. But the situation continued to deteriorate, and it seemed there was little the United States could do: "We picked a bad horse,"[29] said Truman.

Meanwhile, Chiang Kai-shek's rival, Mao Zedong, was gaining popularity. Although Mao received little support from Stalin because Mao rejected the tenets of Marxist-Leninism, many Americans were convinced that he was Stalin's pawn. Others believed that he was acting independently to fight for communism in China. Either way, Mao drew considerable opposition in the United States. Americans worried that Mao was part of an international communist movement that, if successful in China, could easily spread to other parts of the world.

Chiang Kai-shek (above) fought to overthrow communism in his country. Mao Zedong (left) rallies for communism in front of a supportive crowd.

In the fall of 1949, Mao Zedong, using captured Japanese arms, gained control of China. Chiang Kai-shek fled to the island of Formosa. By October 1949, Mao had proclaimed a communist state, the People's Republic of China (PRC). "We, the Chinese people, have now stood up,"[30] he announced. Communism had been victorious in China.

Recently declassified Soviet documents show that the United States overestimated Stalin's relationship with Mao. Stalin only slowly began to think of Mao as a potential ally. According to Russian historians Zubok and Pleshakov, "Only after the beginning of the Cold War, when all chances for reconciliation with the West were lost and he faced the need to find new partners and allies, did Stalin begin to reassess Mao, who then was clearly on the winning side in the war [in China]."[31] By December 1949, Stalin agreed to meet Mao in Moscow, and the two countries drafted a Sino-Soviet treaty of friendship, alliance, and mutual assistance, which was signed later in February 1950. Stalin still did not completely trust Mao, however, and made it clear that the alliance would work only if Mao recognized him as the supreme communist leader.

American politicians were greatly alarmed by Mao's victory in China, and the U.S. government refused to give diplomatic recognition to the new government. As American anxiety over China escalated, prominent political figures such as Senator William Knowland of California, Representative Walter Judd of Minnesota, and publisher Henry Luce tried to blame the Truman administration.

U.S. newspaper headlines proclaimed that the United States had "lost" China. Both Truman and Secretary of State Dean Acheson were heavily criticized for the Chinese nationalists' defeat.

The Communist victory in China's civil war and the founding of the PRC changed the character of the Cold War. The world's largest country in population, consisting of almost 470 million people, now stood solidly in the communist camp. Washington, and soon the rest of America, would decide that the communist threat must be stopped.

NSC-68

Trying to determine his best course of action, Truman asked the State and Defense Departments to "make an overall review and reassessment of American foreign and defense policy in the light of the loss of China."[32] In April 1950, the National Security Council responded with a policy paper whose contents would have far-reaching effects on the Cold War.

The document, NSC-68, urged the president to promote independent and friendly states in Asia to counter Soviet expansionism, arguing that "the social and economic problems faced by the free nations in this area present more than offsetting opportunities for Communist expansion."[33] To a certain extent, the document allowed U.S. policy makers to justify intervention in world affairs as necessary means to halt communism. Historian Stephen Ambrose explains, "The document provided the justification for

COMMUNISTS TAKE CHINA

The following excerpts from a Time *article published February 7, 1949, demonstrate the severe anticommunist attitude that pervaded the United States after communist forces secured power in China.*

"It had been the Year of the Rat—and the year of the Communists. In the Chinese calendar, the old year stood for misfortune and deceit. A few surreptitious firecrackers, still forbidden under martial law, last week heralded the New Year of the Ox, which signified hard work and persistence. In present-day China, inevitably, it also signified sorrow and loss.

Nanking people who remained tried to celebrate the New Year as best they could. In the back rooms of their stores, shopkeepers lit candles on their red altars for ceremonial offerings to the gods. Barbershops were doing a rush business, and fortune tellers were so sought after that they made appointments days in advance. Nanking's miserable colony of refugees from Communist areas was sprinkled with red paper signs asking health & wealth from the gods. An old man who had fled Suchow three months ago tapped tobacco from some cigarette butts into his pipe and said: 'At home in Suchow I would be burning incense to the gods. Now look at me.'

[The city of] Peiping, . . . surrendered to the Reds last fortnight, was nervously expecting the Communists to take over. Anti-Communist signs had been hastily removed from walls; Communist proclamations appeared mysteriously instead. Policemen were especially polite—anyone in the streets might be a Red spy. Out of the open city gates, disarmed Nationalist troops marched by the thousands.

A few days later, 20,000 smartly uniformed Communist troops marched in, with two brass bands. They had left their Russian trucks outside the city, displaying only the U.S. ones which they had captured from Chiang's armies. Picked Nationalist soldiers grimly guarded the Reds' line of march. Beneath pictures of Communist Boss Mao Tse-tung (none of Joseph Stalin), sound trucks blared: Long live the liberation! Crowds watched the Reds in silence."

America's assuming the role of world policeman and came close to saying that all change was directed by Communists and should therefore be resisted."[34]

Even more significant, NSC-68 warned of the Soviet Union's awesome military power, stating that the USSR was "developing the military capacity to support its design for world domination."[35] The report predicted that by 1954 the Soviet Union would have the nuclear weapons to destroy the United States, and recommended an immediate and large-scale buildup of the U.S. military. This would require major increases in defense spending—up to $50 billion per year would be needed to counter the Soviet threat.

The report stunned American policy makers. They knew that they would need the full support of Congress, as well as of the American people, to justify such massive outlays and the tax increases that would be needed as a result. While officials pondered how to market the idea to the public, war broke out in Korea. The war provided justification for building up the military, giving both the American taxpayers and legislators an enemy and a reason to approve increased military spending. "Korea saved us,"[36] Acheson would later remark.

THE KOREAN WAR

The Korean War was the first overt military conflict of the Cold War. Japan had annexed Korea in 1910 and ruled the country until 1945, when the Allies divided the country along the 38th parallel. Shortly after, the Soviet Union supported a communist dictator, Kim Il-Sung, in the North, where Soviet troops were stationed. Likewise, in the Republic of South Korea, the United States sponsored elections in 1948 that put Syngman Rhee in office as president. One year after the elections, U.S. troops left Korea.

On June 24, 1950, Communist North Korean troops invaded South Korea. The Americans assumed immediately that Stalin was the mastermind behind the invasion. U.S. policy makers believed that the Soviet dictator must be stopped in Korea before he moved on to other parts of the world. "The Communists in the Kremlin [the site of the Soviet government] are engaged in a monstrous conspiracy to stamp out freedom all over the world,"[37] Truman explained in an April 1951 address defending U.S. intervention.

In reality, however, the conflict originated as a civil war rather than an international conflict. Kim invaded South Korea because he wanted to reunify the Korean peninsula under the communist flag. Having witnessed the victory of the communists in China, Kim hoped that Korea would be the next country to move toward communism.

Kim did realize that his invasion plan would be more likely to succeed with the help of Stalin. To this end, he had been begging Stalin for support for many months. According to a classified Soviet account, Stalin had held off approval of the invasion although he "did not object in principle." He wrote, "such big business regarding South Korea requires serious preparation."[38] Only when Stalin finally agreed to meet Kim in Moscow in April 1950 did he agree that reunifying Korea was a goal that he was willing to endorse.

Stalin was persuaded to support Kim in large part because he believed that the United States would not intervene in the matter. The Soviet leader wanted to avoid direct military confrontation with the United States, but he interpreted recent events and U.S. officials' statements to mean that the United States was no longer interested in Korea. Afterall, the United States had recently pulled all of its troops out of the country. And when Secretary of State Acheson announced the U.S. containment plan for Asia a few months earlier, he had excluded Korea from the list of Asian nations that the United States would defend. In addition, Stalin had read a Soviet intelligence report, coming from South Korea, that supported his mistaken assumption. The account quoted Syngman Rhee to say, "America has shown from the very beginning that it does not intend to fight for the interests of South Korea."[39] Assured that the United States would not interfere, Stalin decided to support the North Korean aggression, believing that it would strengthen the position of the Soviet Union in Asia and his own prestige worldwide.

However, Stalin miscalculated badly. Truman acted immediately to defend South Korea. He viewed the invasion as a direct threat to Japan and a test of U.S. containment policy in Asia by the Soviets. He believed that failure to respond would pave the way for future Soviet aggression in other parts of the world.

The American president sent arms to South Korea and ordered the attack of North Korea from the air. The U.S. then

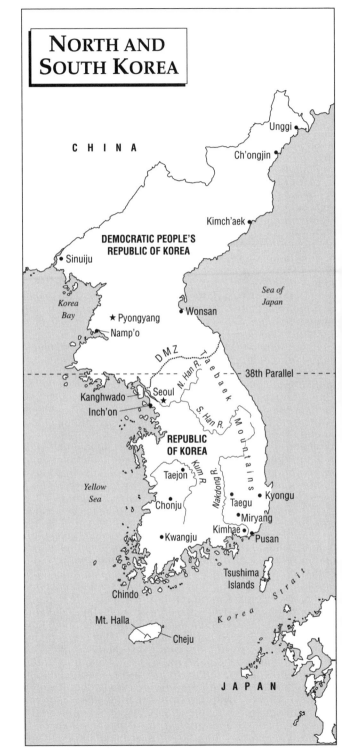

moved on to gain support from the United Nations. The Soviet delegates were not present at the UN Security Council meeting where the idea was introduced because they were boycotting to show their displeasure over UN nonrecognition of China. As a result, the United States was able to acquire UN military commitment to Korea. A few days later, the United Nations sent ground troops into South Korea.

The American and UN response had been swift. By the fall of 1950, UN troops, dominated by American forces, defeated the North Korean troops in South Korea, freed Seoul, the capital of South Korea, and pushed the North Koreans back to the preinvasion border at the 38th parallel. But the fighting was not yet over.

Energized by the successful counterattack, the United States decided that rather than simply containing communism in North Korea, communism could be defeated there entirely and the country reunified under a noncommunist government. Under the leadership of General MacArthur, the United States began air strikes against bridges on the Yulu River, bordering North Korea and China. The destruction of these transportation routes angered the Chinese, who worried that American aggression against communism might move next into China.

American troops sprint out of their helicopters onto an open field during the Korean War.

General MacArthur (left) inspects troops at Kimpo airfield in South Korea.

When MacArthur's troops continued their advance north toward the Chinese border, Mao decided he had had enough. China intervened in the conflict, and a significant escalation of the war ensued. The Chinese and North Korean forces, supported financially and militarily by the USSR, drove the UN troops back toward Seoul. South Korean and American troops suffered considerable losses during this period of the war. The Chinese intervention locked the conflict in a stalemate; armistice talks, continuing for a year and a half, produced no agreements on issues concerning the division of the country and the treatment of prisoners of war. The conflict that had begun as a civil war among Koreans had developed into an international battle between Soviet and Chinese communists and American and Western capitalists. Historians Zubok and Pleshakov write, "In the end, tiny Korea remained in a deadly trilateral embrace, between the United States on one side, determined to beat back world communism, and on the other side, the PRC and the USSR, each guided by . . . the enormous egos of their leaders."[40]

Finally, in July 1953, after a change in leadership in both the United States and the Soviet Union, a permanent cease-fire was reached. Only two weeks after Stalin's death in March, the new Soviet leadership concluded that the war in Korea must be ended. In China, Mao decided the same thing. In May, the new U.S. president, Dwight D. Eisenhower, also decided that the war must come to an end and threatened Beijing with the use of nuclear weapons. By July, the fighting stopped. The Eisenhower administration credited its threat as the reason for the cease-fire, but in fact both China and the Soviet Union were ready to negotiate a final end to the war.

The Korean War had lasting consequences for Asian politics, as well as on the conduct of international affairs. The Korean peninsula was formally divided into two parts, a communist North Korea and a democratic South Korea. Both were ravaged by fighting. The war killed about 3.4 million Koreans, over 1 million Chinese, and over 54,000 Americans. Significantly, the Korean War showed the world that the U.S.-Soviet rivalry was no longer confined to Europe, and that military, as well as diplomatic, conflict between the two could erupt anywhere on the globe. Moreover, relations between the United States and China, already strained, were further embittered by the war. They would continue to be so for generations.

The war also had profound ramifications within the United States. The Korean War had spurred the United States to significantly increase its military arsenal as recommended by NSC-68. This mili-

American soldiers make their way to the firing line in Korea.

MAO ZEDONG

Mao Zedong was the founder and leader of the People's Republic of China from 1949 until 1976. Born into an affluent peasant family, he received a traditional primary education. Later, he left home in order to escape the authority of his father and to study more modern subjects. In 1911, he participated in the revolution that overthrew the Manchu dynasty, and in 1921 he attended the founding meetings of the Chinese Communist Party. He believed in the revolutionary potential of China's peasantry, and after the party's defeat under Chiang Kai-shek in the late 1920s, Mao moved to the countryside, where he began to construct a powerful peasant movement.

Under Mao's leadership, the Chinese communists won control of China after a civil war that lasted from 1946 to 1949. During the 1950s, Mao's Great Leap Forward program, during which the country moved toward a utopian vision of communism, caused economic chaos, famine, and eventually took as many as 30 million Chinese lives. Mao's belief that nuclear war would result in the defeat of capitalism and the victory of communism caused growing tension with Khrushchev. These tensions, combined with Mao's aspirations to become the leader of world communism, led to a major split between the two huge communist powers, the Soviet Union and China. By 1960 the two countries began to reinforce their four-thousand-mile border and in 1969 they fought a deadly battle along the Ussuri River in the Far East. The Sino-Soviet split changed the character of the Cold War, in essence ending the bipolar world and allowing the United States new opportunities, to normalize U.S.- Chinese relations.

tary expansion sparked a spiraling arms race that would be the most terrifying aspect of the Cold War in the years to come. In addition, America had grown increasingly suspicious of the Soviet Union and the threat of communism. This suspicion would become an irrational obsession that dominated American life.

4 The Cold War at Home

By the early 1950s, Cold War anxieties within the United States led many Americans to believe that the Soviets would stop at nothing to take over the world. Concern grew that Soviet spies were entering the country, and that communists were secretly infiltrating the government, the workplace, and even families, aiming to destroy the American way of life. Some politicians played on these fears in order to advance their own careers or agendas. The result was an anti-communist frenzy, called the Red Scare, that dominated America's political and cultural life.

THE BEGINNING OF THE RED SCARE

The Red Scare climaxed in the 1950s, but its roots dated back for decades. Anticommunist sentiment had run high in 1919 and 1920 when the United States had attempted to aid in the defeat of the Red Army in Russia's civil war. At that time U.S. Attorney General A. Mitchell Palmer claimed that communist agents from Russia were planning to overthrow the American government, and on November 7, 1919, the second anniversary of the Russian

Revolution, more than ten thousand suspected communists and anarchists were arrested in what became known as the Palmer Raids. The majority of the suspects were released shortly thereafter, however, and the first "red scare" began to subside.

During World War II, with the United States and the Soviet Union joined in the Allied cause to defeat Nazi Germany, anticommunist sentiment faded even more. In fact, the favorable view of the Soviets contributed to a surge in membership in the American Communist Party, which rose to more than eighty thousand by the early 1940s. Even so, low-level anticommunism remained a factor in American politics. In 1940, for example, Congress passed the Smith Act, which criminalized advocating the overthrow of the U.S. government by force or joining any organization that advocated the same.

Some American politicians manipulated communist paranoia for their own political purposes. In the 1944 presidential campaign, for example, Republican candidate Thomas Dewey warned that the Democratic Party was being taken over by communists, proclaiming, "Vote Republican and keep the communists from running your country and your life."[41] In March 1947, not wanting to be labeled "soft on communism," President Truman launched a loyalty probe of the U.S. government, ordering the investigation of more than 3 million government employees for communist sympathies. Truman's order came during the same week that he delivered his speech to Congress outlining the Truman Doctrine. His exaggerated rhetoric in the speech heightened public anxiety.

Also in 1947, The House Un-American Activities Committee (HUAC) accelerated its activities in searching for communists and other subversives in the United States. Founded in 1937, the committee aimed to investigate "the extent, character, and objects of un-American propaganda activities in the United States, [and] the diffusion within the United States of subversive and un-American propaganda."[42] The committee began to take a special interest in finding communists in the entertainment business, in universities, and in government.

By 1950 the federal government was discharging people from governmental service as potential security risks. Although many of those discharged were eccentric in some way, most were without a doubt loyal to the United States. Many others were seen as guilty through association. Before long, people began pointing fingers, accusing one another of being, as Truman called them, "reds, phonies, and parlor pinks."[43]

In Hollywood, HUAC dedicated itself to finding communist sympathizers among the celebrities of the motion picture industry. When ten prominent screenwriters and directors refused to testify before the committee, they were jailed. Hundreds of others in the entertainment industry were blacklisted, their careers ruined because of their political views or simply because they invoked their Fifth Amendment rights in testimony before the committee. Popular movies, such as *Mission to Moscow* (1943) and *Song of Russia* (1944), which had been produced during World War II when the United States and Soviet Union were Allies, were now condemned. Some American filmmakers realized that their careers were at stake and rushed to make pro-American, anticommunist films.

FEAR OF INTERNAL SPIES

HUAC also exposed alleged communists within the federal government. America's anticommunist frenzy intensified in 1948 when HUAC named Alger Hiss, a former State Department official, as a communist agent. Hiss had had an exemplary career, having worked as one of FDR's closest advisers. In fact, Hiss had personally briefed Roosevelt before the crucial Yalta conference toward the end of World War II. Republican representative Richard M. Nixon, of California, led the questioning of Hiss before the House committee.

Hiss's strong allies in the Truman administration, including Secretary of State Acheson and Truman himself, supported him in refuting the allegations. Later, however, evidence was found linking Hiss to classified documents that had been turned over to the Soviets. Although his first trial ended in a hung jury, Hiss was retried in 1950 and found guilty of perjury.

Richard Nixon (left) points out the headline that reads of Alger Hiss's guilty verdict. Hiss (below) denies allegations of communist involvement before the House Committee on Un-American Activities.

Protesting his innocence, Hiss served forty-four months in federal prison. To this day debate over Hiss's guilt continues. In 1992, the *New York Times* reported that a high-ranking Russian official claimed that newly opened archives cleared Alger Hiss of charges that he spied for the Soviet Union. Hiss, at eighty-seven years old, responded to the news from his New York City apartment, saying, "It's been what I've been fighting for, for 44 years."[44]

The Hiss case was important not only because it fueled the growing anticommunist hysteria in the country, but also because it demonstrated that some politicians would exploit anticommunism for their own political gains. Nixon, for example, had quickly ascertained that the Republicans could gain political ground by attacking Democrats for underestimat-

J. Edgar Hoover

J. Edgar Hoover was appointed director of the Bureau of Investigations, a somewhat shadowy government agency, in 1924. Hoover swiftly turned the agency, which was renamed the Federal Bureau of Investigation (FBI) in 1935, into a well-known and respected organization prominent in the field of domestic intelligence and espionage. Hoover created a centralized fingerprint file, a crime laboratory, and the National Police Academy.

After World War II, Hoover spoke out as an ardent anticommunist, and he led the FBI to conduct a dedicated anticommunist campaign within the United States. The FBI kept files on many Americans, including congressmen and politicians, and it carried out investigations of anyone suspected to be either a communist sympathizer or a spy.

A strict conservative, J. Edgar Hoover rarely socialized with others. His daily life was routine and dedicated to work. Each morning he was driven to the office; often he chose to walk the last few blocks. In the evenings he indulged in one drink on his balcony before dinner. Hoover was one of the most influential figures in Washington politics, directing the FBI for an impressive forty-eight years until his death in 1972.

J. Edgar Hoover speaks out against communism. Hoover directed the Federal Bureau of Investigation for forty-eight years.

ing the communist threat. His role in the Hiss case, in fact, served to catapult his career, which culminated in his election to the presidency in 1968. Nixon later wrote of the fame the case brought him:

I received considerable credit for spearheading the investigation which led to Hiss's conviction. Two years later I was elected to the U.S. Senate and two years after that General Eisenhower introduced me as his running mate to the Republican national convention as "a man who has a special talent and an ability to ferret out any kind of subversive influence wherever it may be found, and the strength and persistence to get rid of it."[45]

The director of the Federal Bureau of Investigation (FBI), J. Edgar Hoover, a powerful force behind the anticommunist fever, also took advantage of public fears to build his career. Hoover saw that by focusing on the removal of spies and communists in the country, he could increase the scope and status of the FBI. Under Hoover's command, FBI agents set out to weed out internal communists from the American landscape. They used unjustified and even illegal tactics to gather evidence, including break-ins, phone taps, and bugs.

In this environment, neighbors were encouraged to spy on one another, and children and parents were praised for reporting each other's statements and actions. Although much of this evidence was inadmissible in court, the cultivation of informants contributed to highly charged atmosphere of deception and mistrust. Using inflammatory rhetoric to describe the threat of communism, Hoover invoked fear and concern among fellow Americans: "Communism, in reality, is not a political party, it is a way of life, an evil and malignant way of life. It reveals a condition akin to disease that spreads like an epidemic and like an epidemic a quarantine is necessary to keep it from infecting this nation."[46]

Although the situation was clearly overblown, Soviet spies did exist on American territory. In January 1950, German-born British nuclear physicist Klaus Fuchs was arrested in London for espionage. Fuchs had worked at the U.S. Atomic Research Laboratory in Los Alamos, New Mexico; he confessed to giving atomic secrets to the Soviets and named a number of American accomplices. He was sentenced to fourteen years in prison.

The investigation of Fuchs's accomplices led to the arrest of Julius and Ethel Rosenberg in New York City. The Rosenbergs, both members of the Communist Party, were convicted of giving atomic secrets to the Soviets during World War II. Although the case against Ethel was particularly weak, the FBI hoped that threatening her with prosecution would convince Julius to talk about his spying activities, potentially naming other spies. Julius refused. After two years of appeals, and despite protests that the Rosenbergs were victims of anticommunist hysteria, the couple were executed in New York State's Sing Sing prison in 1953.

Naturally, Americans spied on the Soviets as well. The U.S. government founded the Central Intelligence Agency in 1947 to gather information on other

Ethel and Julius Rosenberg leave the federal court after being convicted of revealing atomic bomb secrets to the Soviets.

countries and conduct undercover operations. The CIA built a tunnel in Berlin in 1955 that stretched five hundred yards to a point not far from Soviet military headquarters in East Berlin. Stationed in comfortable and soundproofed chambers, American agents eavesdropped on top-secret Soviet communications until the tunnel was discovered in 1956. American spies also took to the air; in the 1950s and 1960s, the United States flew more than ten thousand spy missions, many into Soviet airspace.

But the Americans seemed less successful in recruiting agents than the Soviets. The Soviet spy network, run by the secret police, or the Committee for State Security (KGB), and the Soviet military intelligence agency, the Chief Directorate of Intelligence (GRU), was probably the largest in the world. Certainly one of its greatest successes was gaining access to American information on building the atomic bomb.

THE RED SCARE AND MCCARTHYISM

Amid the prosecutions of Hiss, Fuchs, and the Rosenbergs, public fear of internal communists reached new heights. On February 9, 1950, Republican Senator Joseph R.

THE COLD WAR HITS HOLLYWOOD

The Red Scare and McCarthyism had a profound effect on American cinema of the time. The first major anticommunist film was *The Iron Curtain* (1948), which told the story of a clerk at the Russian embassy in Ottawa, Canada, who decided to defect to the West. A rash of films followed, often depicting the exposure of Communist Party members or spies in America, including *I Married a Communist* (1950) and *My Son John* (1952). Other well-known movies of the era involving Cold War conflicts included *The Red Danube* (1950) and *Big Jim McClain* (1952). In *Big Jim McClain* famous western movie hero John Wayne played a HUAC investigator pursuing Communists in Hawaii.

Meanwhile Hollywood filmmakers who wanted to make a political statement about the Cold War had to disguise their plots in unusual settings. Westerns, for example, became a forum in which rivals, such as Native Americans and white settlers, could work out their differences. *Storm Center* (1956), starring Bette Davis, was perhaps the only film during the 1950s to speak out directly against McCarthyism. By the 1960s, however, after the Red Scare had subsided, filmmakers enjoyed greater liberties and Hollywood movies took on a more sophisticated view of the Cold War. Many movies, such as the black comedy *Dr. Strangelove* (1963), addressed the terrifying issue of nuclear warfare in absurdist terms.

McCarthy of Wisconsin gave a speech in West Virginia in which he claimed that more than two hundred communists had infiltrated the State Department. McCarthy claimed, "The reason why we find ourselves in a position of impotency is not because our only powerful potential enemy has sent men to invade our shores, but rather because of the traitorous actions of those who have been treated so well by this Nation. . . . In my opinion the State Department, which is one of the most important government departments, is thoroughly infested with Communists."[47] He went on to accuse Secretary of State Dean Acheson of being one of the most dangerous subversives, a "pompous diplomat in striped pants, with a phony British accent."[48]

McCarthy and other Republicans used anticommunist attacks to discredit the Democrats and promote their own party. In a telegram that McCarthy sent later that week to Truman, he criticized the president for not eliminating "security risks because of communist connections in the government. . . . I would suggest, therefore, Mr. President, that you simply pick up your phone and ask Mr. Acheson how many of those whom your board had labeled as dangerous he failed to discharge." He concluded by alluding to the political ramifications the Democrats might suffer, adding, "Failure on your part will label the Democratic party of being the bed-fellow of international communism."[49]

McCarthy was appointed to chair the Senate Committee on Operations, a position that gave him a forum from which to continue his crusade. McCarthy led the committee during the next two years, subpoenaing people to testify about their political views and their political past. He presented lists of alleged communists, and engaged in vicious verbal attacks on people, usually unfounded, based on their political views. After admitting connections to the Communist Party, many people lost their jobs.

In March 1951, HUAC revived its investigation of potential communists in the entertainment industry, causing great alarm in Hollywood. Many studio bosses pledged not to employ anyone associated with the Communist Party. Those who looked the other way were quickly blacklisted, including some of the industry's most talented directors, writers, and actors. Others went into exile abroad, or worked in Hollywood under false names.

McCarthy also targeted universities in his anticommunist crusade. While no formal blacklist emerged, universities investigated the political backgrounds of their employees, condemning anyone associated with left-leaning politics. J. Edgar Hoover disparaged America's teachers and professors calling them "reducators" that were "creating doubts in the validity of the American way of life."[50] Such comments added to the hysteria in which thousands of professors and others lost their academic jobs.

Senator Joseph McCarthy (right) listens as his assistant Roy Cohn whispers during an anti-communism hearing.

McCarthy also targeted what he believed to be anti-American literature. His staff investigated the State Department's overseas libraries, discovering thirty thousand allegedly procommunist books that were then removed from the shelves. In addition, McCarthy's supporters pursued communists in the United Nations, where many American staff members either left or were dismissed. As in other sectors of the American workforce, it was easier for bosses to fire those under suspicion than to look the other way and therefore come under suspicion themselves.

Despite McCarthy's deplorable methods, there was significant support for his cause both in the American public and among policy makers. In early 1950, Congress passed the Internal Security Act over the president's veto. This act made it unlawful for anyone to "contribute to the establishment . . . of a totalitarian dictator."[51] In 1951 the Supreme Court upheld the Smith Act convictions of eleven Communist Party leaders on charges of conspiring to organize as the Communist Party and to teach Marxist-Leninism. The men served three to five years in federal prison and paid fines of $10,000. Further charges followed, with as many as 140 Communist Party leaders indicted in the United States simply because of their political views.

Although many politicians joined McCarthy's crusade, some, including fellow Republicans, condemned McCarthy as a witch-hunter. A Senate subcommittee established to investigate McCarthy's claims found that it was "clearly apparent that the charges of Communist infiltration of and influence upon the State Department are false. This knowledge is reassuring to all Americans whose faith has been temporarily shaken in the security of their Government by perhaps the most nefarious campaign of untruth in the history of our Republic."[52]

McCarthy's anticommunist campaign probably helped the Republicans win the 1952 presidential elections, and the senator continued his crusade even after the Truman administration had left office. He accused General George Marshall, greatly revered in the United States and architect of the Marshall Plan, of procommunism, as "part of a conspiracy so immense, an infamy so black, as to dwarf any in the history of man."[53] When President Eisenhower failed to defend the general, former president Truman remarked:

> It is now evident that the present administration has fully embraced, for political advantage, McCarthyism. I am not referring to the Senator from Wisconsin. He is important in that his name has taken on the dictionary meaning of the word. It is the corruption of truth, the abandonment of due process of law. It is the use of the big lie and the unfounded accusation against any citizen in the name of Americanism or security.[54]

The Senate subcommittee's findings and Truman's remarks helped convince the American public and prominent policy makers that McCarthy had gone too far. In time, his anticommunist tirades were brought to an end. During Senate hearings that were broadcast live on national televi-

An Interview with Former Spy and Retired KGB Major General Oleg Kalugin

Oleg Kalugin was a major figure in the Soviet intelligence agency, the KGB. Kalugin first traveled to the United States in 1958 as a student and fledgling spy. He spent thirty-two years in the KGB, first playing a major role in spy rings, and later as chief of KGB foreign counterintelligence and a major general. Kalugin retired from the KGB in 1990, after agitating for its reform. After the breakup of the Soviet Union, Kalugin served briefly as a people's deputy to the Russian parliament. In the following interview, archived at the CNN Cold War website, Kalugin discusses some of the goals of the KGB:

"The chief mission of the intelligence, as defined by the Soviet leadership, was to forewarn the Soviet leadership of impending military crises.... As you know, the Soviet leadership was paranoid about a potential Western attack against the U.S.S.R., and for that reason the intelligence [agencies were] given all they wanted [in order] to provide the leadership with advance warning about forthcoming events.

On the other hand—and this is the other side of the Soviet intelligence, very important: perhaps I would describe it as the heart and soul of the Soviet intelligence—was subversion. Not intelligence collection, but subversion: active measures to weaken the West, to drive wedges in the Western community alliances of all sorts, particularly NATO, to sow discord among allies, to weaken the United States in the eyes of the people of Europe, Asia, Africa, Latin America, and thus to prepare ground in case the war really occurs. To make America more vulnerable to the anger and distrust of other peoples....

It was ruthless in Stalin's times, and the measure of its ruthlessness—well, it's of a historic proportion. I think if we compare Hitler to Stalin, and the Gestapo to the KGB, the KGB was far more ruthless—not because they killed far more people, but because they were indiscriminate in the selection of victims. After Stalin's death, the KGB underwent serious reforms, but not serious enough to declare it a legitimate organization abiding by the laws of the state. In fact, it was a tool in the hands of the totalitarian state, in the hands of the Soviet leadership. And it was used at their will."

sion in 1954, McCarthy claimed that communism had now infiltrated the U.S. Army. As millions of Americans watched, Army counsel Joseph N. Welsh famously challenged McCarthy: "Mr. Senator... you have done enough.... At long last, have you left no sense of decency?"[55] The gallery applauded with relief. Someone had finally stood up to the senator. In December 1954 the Senate voted to condemn McCarthy for bringing that body into disrepute.

A mother watches the McCarthy-Army hearings in 1954. Anticommunist fever waned after the U.S. Senate put an end to McCarthy's tactics.

After McCarthy's disgrace, the anticommunist hysteria gradually settled down. But the impact of the crusade left a deep scar on the American people and their culture. Movies, television, and books would continue to take an anticommunist tone. Many ordinary people remained too scared to openly express their political viewpoints. Ironically, the Red Scare had shown that while the United States championed the protection of democracy and freedom for people abroad, it had permitted an era of fear and intolerance to violate those very freedoms at home.

Chapter

5 New Leaders Provide a Possible Respite

In 1953, new leaders entered the White House and the Kremlin, and a new phase in the Cold War began. Dwight D. Eisenhower, enormously popular in the United States, seemed poised to forge more friendly relations with the Soviet Union. Likewise, in Moscow, the death of Stalin ushered in a new leadership with Nikita Khrushchev, and the potential for new approaches and better relations. The outlooks of the two superpower leaders initially did allow tensions to ease. By 1960, however, new policies in the Soviet Union and United States had allowed crises to develop in Hungary and Egypt and sparked a nuclear arms race that threatened the entire globe. The Cold War had been revived.

EISENHOWER'S NEW LOOK

The accusation that communists had infiltrated the Truman government certainly helped Eisenhower to garner votes during the 1952 presidential campaign. Although Eisenhower remained silent on the issue, his running mate, Richard Nixon, did not. Nixon even went so far as to call Democratic presidential candidate Adlai Steven-son, "Adlai the appeaser ... [with] a Ph.D. from Dean Acheson's College of Cowardly Communist Containment."[56]

But anticommunist sentiment alone did not bring the Republicans to the White House. The Eisenhower-Nixon ticket appealed to the American voters for a number of other reasons. First and foremost, Eisenhower was a person the American voters felt they could trust. Having commanded the Allied forces in World War II, Eisenhower was an authentic military hero who displayed honesty, loyalty, and simplicity. His folksy and low-key style greatly appealed to the American people and earned him the nickname "smiling Ike." His war experiences demonstrated that he understood hard work, courage, and worldly matters. Voters accepted the Republican campaign slogan "It's time for a change,"[57] giving Eisenhower a landslide victory with 34 million popular votes.

Once he took office, Eisenhower promised to be "conservative when it comes to money and liberal when it comes to human beings."[58] In keeping with this promise, Eisenhower approached the Cold War with the priority of minimizing costs. His "New Look" policy emphasized air power and nuclear

Dwight D. Eisenhower (left) and a friend prepare to take off for a flight. Eisenhower was popular with the American public for his honesty and simplicity.

weapons rather than conventional weapons and ground troops, a strategy aimed at trimming the budget and reducing taxes while maintaining a strong defense. According to historian Stephen E. Ambrose, "The New Look rejected the premise of NSC-68 that the United States could spend up to 20 percent of its GNP on arms; it rejected deficit spending; it supported a policy of containment."[59]

Eisenhower relied on his secretary of state, John Foster Dulles, to shape the administration's foreign policy. A well-educated man, Dulles had an impressive professional resume that included positions as foreign affairs adviser to President Woodrow Wilson, presidential candidate Thomas Dewey, and President Harry Tru-

man. In that role he had assisted Truman in establishing the United Nations and negotiating the postwar peace treaty with Japan. Now, as secretary of state, Dulles was concerned about alienating the influential right wing of the Republican Party. Although Eisenhower aimed to improve the United States' relationship with the Soviet Union, Dulles knew that the administration would need to take a strong view against communism to win the approval of conservative Republicans.

To achieve this goal, Dulles hoped to support containment yet move beyond it. Dulles coined new phrases calling for an aggressive plan based on the concepts of "liberation," "deterrence," and "massive retaliation." Liberation promised American support for countries that were struggling against communism. In testimony before the Senate Foreign Relations Committee in January 1953, Dulles outlined the importance of liberation, explaining, "We shall never have a secure peace or a happy world so long as Soviet communism dominates one-third of all the people that there are, and is in the process of trying at least to extend its rule to many others.... Therefore, we must always have in mind the liberation of these captive peoples."[60]

Secretary of State John Foster Dulles arrives in London to discuss the Suez Crisis with leaders from Britain and France.

Dulles also focused on the deterrence, or prevention, of Soviet aggression. He said that in contrast to the passive policy of containment, which had focused on the American response to Soviet actions, the current policy would proactively deter communist aggression while keeping military costs low. The new strategy, relying on strategic air power and nuclear weapons, would prove not only cost-effective but also less dangerous for American soldiers.

Massive retaliation meant that the United States threatened to meet any communist aggression with the nuclear annihilation of the Soviet Union. Dulles called the overall approach "brinkmanship." Brinkmanship meant that the United States would refuse to back down in the face of a crisis, even if it might mean going to war. Explaining the policy, Dulles said, "You have to take chances on peace, just as you must take chances in war.... The ability to get [to] the verge without getting into war is the necessary art.... If you try to run away from it, if you are scared to go to the brink, you are lost."[61]

Despite the toughness of deterrence and massive retaliation, Eisenhower was not fully comfortable in the position of hardline cold warrior and worried about the prospects of a nuclear war. Smiling Ike hoped that the political situation was loosening up in Russia, and that now was the time to forge a safer and more peaceful understanding between the two nations.

KHRUSHCHEV'S THAW

Six weeks after Eisenhower was sworn in as president, Joseph Stalin died, and

THE THAW IN SOVIET LITERATURE

Under Stalin, Soviet literature was highly controlled and censored. The Communist Party favored literature that praised the new Soviet man, glorified Stalin, and displayed a mistrust of foreigners. After Khrushchev came to power, however, Soviet writers were permitted greater freedom and authors began to openly condemn and criticize Stalin. In his 1954 book *The Thaw* Ilya Ehrenburg was one of the first writers to denounce Stalin. By 1962, it seemed that the controls on literature were loosened even further, as Khrushchev himself approved the publication of Alexander Solzhenitsyn's *One Day in the Life of Ivan Denisovich*, another book that exposed the evils of Stalin and his prison camp system. The official approval was remarkable because Solzhenitsyn had spent eight years in Soviet labor camps for his writings after World War II. Poetry also experienced the thaw in censorship. Yevgeny Yevtushenko's poems, again with the approval of Khrushchev, criticized the Stalin period.

There were limits to the freedom, however, as Boris Pasternak found out. Published abroad, Pasternak's *Dr. Zhivago* was viewed by the Soviets as antisocialist. When the author won the Nobel Prize in 1958, Pasternak was prevented from traveling abroad to receive his award. Despite the success of *One Day in the Life of Ivan Denisovich*, Solzhenitsyn's later works were also not appreciated by the Soviet authorities. Solzhenitsyn's *The First Circle*, *Cancer Ward*, and *The Gulag Archipelago*, all critical of the Soviet

regime, were published abroad. In fact, because of his writings, Solzhenitsyn was stripped of Soviet citizenship and exiled in 1974.

Those writers who could not get their works published by the official Soviet publishing houses resorted to "samizdat" (self-publishing) or underground publishing houses. After Gorbachev came to power in 1985, glasnost brought an end to most restrictions on literature.

Boris Pasternak won the Nobel Prize for literature in 1958 but was not allowed to leave the Soviet Union to accept his award.

Nikita Khrushchev addresses the General Assembly of the United Nations. Daily life in the Soviet Union relaxed after Khrushchev became the nation's leader.

Nikita Khrushchev, a member of Stalin's inner circle, eventually emerged as the new leader. Khrushchev and others forged a more open path in Soviet politics, both at home and abroad, and the Communist Party control loosened.

Khrushchev's early years in power have often been called "the thaw," as many aspects of Soviet daily life seemed to relax. Writers and artists, in particular, experienced greater freedom to depict and criticize the Soviet reality. Political persecution, which had become a normal part of everyday life under Stalin, eased considerably. Almost immediately after coming to power, Khrushchev greatly reduced the number of forced labor camps and freed tens of thousands of political prisoners. In addition, average Soviet citizens no longer lived in fear that the secret police were watching their every move.

The highlight of Khrushchev's thaw was the 20th Congress of the Communist Party in February 1956. During a six-hour speech, Nikita Khrushchev denounced Stalin and his reign of terror. He condemned Stalin's crimes and called Stalin a "flawed leader" who had acted like a criminal. He said that "after the war . . . Stalin became even more capricious, irritable, and brutal; in particular, his suspicion grew. His persecution mania reached unbelievable dimensions. Many workers were becoming enemies before his very eyes. . . . He decided everything alone, without any consideration for anyone or anything."[62] Coming only three years after Stalin's death, the denunciation was stunning, domestically and internationally. By exposing and condemning Stalin's horrors, Khrushchev suggested that the years of fear and suspicion had finally come to an end.

This historic speech was remarkable not only because of the condemnation of Stalin. Khrushchev also spoke of an easing of tensions with the United States. He rejected the inevitability of war between the two superpowers and between the capitalist and communist systems, saying, "At the present time, the situation has changed radically. . . . War is not fatalistically inevitable."[63] Khrushchev believed that the Cold War was a transition period in the path to "peaceful coexistence" and economic cooperation. According to historians Zubok and Pleshakov, "The future, in Khrushchev's opinion, would be a cold peace perhaps, but hardly the Cold War."[64]

Khrushchev felt challenged, at least initially, to bring about this peaceful coexistence more quickly. He set his hopes on a new generation of leaders that would acknowledge the Soviet Union's rightful place in the world. With this in mind, he made a number of official visits to different countries to forge personal relationships with other world leaders. He traveled to China, Yugoslavia, Britain, France, Indonesia, and even, in 1959, to the United States. He also dissolved Cominform, the organization Stalin created in 1947 to ensure communist loyalty among the satellite states in Eastern Europe. Khrushchev's actions seemed to prove that Moscow was now more open to the rest of the world.

CRISES IN EASTERN EUROPE AND THE MIDDLE EAST

In Eastern Europe, Khrushchev's famous speech and the dissolution of Cominform sparked a call for change. Shortly after the speech, Poland's Communist Party leader died, and Polish workers were emboldened to demand improved living conditions. Riots erupted, but the situation was quickly calmed when the Soviets approved activist Wladyslaw Gomulka as the new Polish leader. Gomulka, a communist whose call for greater autonomy for Poland had led to his imprisonment under Stalin in 1951, was a national hero. Released following Stalin's death, Gomulka was both a communist and Polish nationalist; thus, he was now the perfect candidate to lead Poland. Khrushchev accepted Gomulka as the new leader of Poland under the condition that Poland would remain a firm ally of the Soviet Union and a member of the Warsaw Pact.

But the groundswell of discontent had already moved beyond Poland. In October 1956, student demonstrations erupted in Budapest, the capital of Hungary. As the Hungarian police tried to control the situation, workers joined the angry students to topple a huge statue of Stalin. Soviet troops entered Budapest to seal off the city but the discontent quickly spread to other parts of the country. The Soviet and Hungarian Communist Party leaders frantically looked for a solution. They hoped to find a new leader for Hungary who was both nationalist and communist, mirroring the solution that had worked in Poland.

The Soviet authorities chose Igre Nagy, a reformer who had served as Hungary's premier from 1953 to 1955. After Nagy took control, unrest subsided. The new leader announced amnesty for political prisoners and invited noncommunists into his government. After Nagy reassured Moscow that Hungary would remain loyal to the Soviet bloc, Khrushchev withdrew Soviet troops from Budapest in late October.

But on November 1, Nagy announced that Hungary would leave the Warsaw Pact and become a neutral country. He also appealed to the United Nations for aid. Moscow was stunned. This level of autonomy exceeded anything the Kremlin was willing to allow. Two days later some twenty thousand Soviet troops and twenty-five hundred Soviet tanks rolled back into Budapest. Nagy, refusing to relent to the Soviets, announced over Radio Budapest, "Today, at daybreak, Soviet troops attacked our capital with the obvious intent of overthrowing the lawful democratic Hungarian government."[65]

Fighting ensued for the next two weeks. Nearly 700 Soviet soldiers and officers were killed and 1,500 wounded. Between 3,000 and 4,000 Hungarians were killed. Eventually the uprising was stopped, with 200,000 Hungarians fleeing to the West, most crossing the border into Austria. Over the next few months, János Kádár, the new Soviet pick to lead Hungary, reimposed a hard-line Soviet command. The country was again firmly under Khrushchev's control. Nagy, along

Polish President Wladyslaw Gomulka (right) and Khrushchev at the United Nations headquarters in New York.

with three hundred leaders of the rebellion, was later executed.

The Hungarian uprising of 1956 was significant for many reasons. Despite the thaw, it was now clear that Moscow would not allow full autonomy in its satellite states in Eastern Europe. And although he had denounced Stalin as a cruel totalitarian, it was apparent that Khrushchev himself would not hesitate to use brute force when needed to control Eastern Europe.

The world also learned that the United States would not help countries struggling for emancipation from Soviet rule. The Hungarian dissidents had been encouraged not only by Khrushchev's speech and by the success of Poland's reformers, but also by America's Radio Free Europe broadcasts which had led them to believe that the United States would come to their assistance. Eisenhower's liberation policy supported that promise. But when the dissidents received no tangible support from the United States, the liberation policy seemed nothing more than an empty phrase. While it supported the concept of liberation in theory, the United States was

Soviet tanks sit in the center of Budapest, Hungary during the anticommunist uprising in 1956.

U.S.-Soviet Spy Exchange

On May 1, 1960, a U-2 spy plane piloted by Francis Gary Powers was shot down in the Soviet Union. The incident had an extremely negative impact on Soviet-American relations. When the Americans claimed they had no knowledge of the plane, the Soviets called their bluff by sending pictures of the American pilot, now alive in Soviet captivity. Powers was charged with espionage, tried in a Soviet court, and sentenced to three years in prison and seven additional years in Soviet labor camps. However, Powers served for only seventeen months before he was exchanged for Colonel Rudolph Abel, a Soviet spy apprehended in the United States. Gary Powers returned to the United States as an American hero but later grew bitter and highly critical of the CIA. In his memoirs, he writes that he felt as though he was simply a political pawn in a Cold War chess game.

simply not willing to risk war with the Soviets for the freedom of Eastern Europeans. Eastern Europe was firmly enclosed behind the Iron Curtain.

The United States was unresponsive to the situation in Eastern Europe in part because its attention was focused on another crisis unraveling in the Middle East. Planning to build a large hydroelectric dam on the Nile River, Egyptian leader Gamal Abdel Nasser needed financing for the project. When the United States rejected his appeal for aid, Nasser seized control of the Suez Canal from its British owners. He claimed that he needed the income from the canal to pay for the dam project. This seizure outraged the British and its close ally France, and the two countries planned retaliation. In addition, because Nasser had sponsored vicious terrorist at-

tacks against Israel, the Jewish state that had been carved out of Palestine in 1948, Israel was happy to join in the campaign against the Arab ruler.

When Israel, Britain, and France launched an aggressive attack against Egypt in October 1956, the United States was furious. The Eisenhower administration had a hard time believing that its close allies had attacked without American consent. After all, the United States had great influence in the region. American companies had significant holdings in the Arab oil industry, and Eisenhower did not want to sever Arab connections. However, because of a powerful Jewish lobby in the United States, the administration did not want to anger Israel, either. Caught in this bind, the United States pressured the British and their allies to withdraw. The allies complied, but relations between them and the United States were severely strained.

The Soviet Union benefited greatly from the Suez crisis. Khrushchev gained prestige in the Arab world by threatening military strikes against Britain, France, and Israel. Once the crisis subsided, the Soviets offered Egypt the needed financing to build Nasser's dam. Soviet prestige and influence rose sharply in Egypt while America's faltered. In addition, the crisis gave the Soviets the perfect opportunity to move troops into Budapest while Western attention was focused on the Middle East.

In reaction to the course of events, the United States vowed to expand containment. In 1957 the United States adopted the Eisenhower Doctrine, which committed U.S. military force, if needed, to contain communism in the Middle East. The Cold War had spread to the Middle East.

SPUTNIK AND THE MISSILE RACE

The conflicts in Hungary and Egypt had exposed the fact that, despite new leaders and fresh approaches, underlying tensions still remained between the Soviet Union and the United States. However, it was in outer space where Cold War rivalry was truly revived. On October 4, 1957, the Soviet Union launched *Sputnik*, the world's first man-made satellite.

The launching of *Sputnik* came as an immense shock to America. Suddenly, or so it seemed, Soviet technology had surpassed that of the United States in a field in which American superiority was taken for granted. Calling into question the quality of American science, *Sputnik* brought about a feeling of national embarrassment. In 1958, Eisenhower set up the National Aeronautics and Space Administration (NASA) and the agency quickly began working on options for a manned space flight, with the aim of getting a man on the moon before the Soviets did.

The military implications of *Sputnik* were even more alarming. The development had come only a few months after the Soviets had announced that they had fired the world's first intercontinental ballistic missile (ICBM). Now, *Sputnik* gave the Soviets the capability to launch ICBMs far from Soviet territory. Carrying nuclear warheads, the missiles could easily reach American targets. Americans were not only inferior in the development of rocket technology, but also vulnerable to nuclear attack.

Sputnik sparked not only the beginning of the space race but also an acceleration of the nuclear arms race between the two countries. The arms race reached terrifying new levels in the 1950s as both sides developed hydrogen, or thermonuclear, bombs. The potency of the new hydrogen bombs was unprecedented, hundreds of times more powerful than the atomic bombs that had been dropped on Japan. Both countries developed nuclear weapons, and as the Cold War continued, both countries stockpiled increasing numbers of these weapons in an effort to outdo the other. Whereas the United States had only 298 atomic bomb in 1950, by 1955 it had 2,422 nuclear weapons. By 1962 this number would grow to 27,100.

To keep up in the arms race, the United States felt it needed current and detailed information about Soviet capabilities. Spy flight missions in high-altitude Lockheed U-2 jets, outfitted with powerful cameras and other electronic equipment to detect radio and radar transmissions, began to fly high over Russia. And although the U-2 spy planes indicated that the Soviets had installed only a limited number of ICBMs, Eisenhower's critics declared that the United States had fallen behind in the missile race. The so-called missile gap was untrue; Air Force General Nathan Twining told Eisenhower, "Everyone knows we already have a [nuclear] stockpile large enough to completely obliterate the Soviet Union."[66]

Nonetheless, the idea that the United States was losing the missile race caused a great uproar in America.

Against his better judgment, Eisenhower succumbed to pressure and ordered an acceleration of the U.S. missile program. In 1958 he revised the 1959 budget to allocate over half of the federal resources, or more than $40 billion, to defense spending. The results were significant. By 1960, the United States enjoyed an overwhelming lead in the missile race in terms of both number and accuracy. In addition, U.S. technology had produced a fleet of submarines that could launch missiles.

For his part, Khrushchev, since the beginning of his term, had been concerned about the American military and technical

An armed soldier stands guard in front of British headquarters in Ismailiya during the Suez crisis.

FEAR OF NUCLEAR WAR

In the United States, the spiraling nuclear arms race fueled an increasing fear of a nuclear attack. Americans began to prepare for the assault, believing that they might actually survive the explosion of a nuclear bomb. Schoolchildren were taught to "duck and cover" their heads should they hear the air-raid warning sirens or if they saw a white flash of a nuclear bomb. In the late 1950s the U.S. government began rapidly building nuclear air-raid shelters. Soon the yellow-and-black sign became a familiar marker in every city in America indicating that the building or structure could be used as shelter in the event of nuclear attack. In addition, families were encouraged to purchase their own private prefabricated shelters.

superiority. Thus, after the Soviets tested their first hydrogen bomb in 1953, Khrushchev supported the development of further technology. He still envisioned a more peaceful world, however. Later he said "We could never possibly use these [nuclear] weapons, but all the same we must be prepared. Our understanding is not a sufficient answer to the arrogance of the imperialists."[67] Khrushchev came to play an active part in the missile race. He attempted to convince the Americans that the Soviet arsenal was much larger than it actually was. In 1957, for example, he announced to the world media that the Soviet Union was turning out missiles as quickly and numerous as sausages on an assembly line.

When Americans began flying U-2 planes through Soviet airspace, Khrushchev warned that this action was intolerable. On June 24, 1956, he cautioned Twining, "Stop sending intruders into our air space. We will shoot down all uninvited guests."[68] In May 1960 the Russians kept their word, bringing down a U-2 spy plane that had been flying high above their territory. At a U.S.-Soviet summit in Paris, Khrushchev demanded that the Americans stop covert flights over Soviet territory. He also insisted that Eisenhower issue an immediate apology. When Eisenhower refused, Khrushchev stormed out of the meetings. With the lines of communication newly frozen, it seemed that the Cold War had been freshly revived.

Chapter

6 Cold War Nightmares: Tensions Escalate

During the administration of President John F. Kennedy, the United States adopted a more confrontational position with respect to the Soviet Union in an attempt to win the Cold War. Meanwhile, in the Soviet Union, Khrushchev was coming under attack from the Communist Party for being too lenient with the Americans. As the two leaders struggled to toughen their responses to each other, Cold War tensions escalated into crises in Berlin and Cuba, and into war in Vietnam.

PRESIDENT KENNEDY'S FLEXIBLE RESPONSE

When Kennedy took office in 1961, he promised a fresh approach to foreign affairs. Criticizing the Eisenhower administration for relying too heavily on nuclear weapons, Kennedy called for an increased role for conventional forces. Kennedy and his advisers replaced Eisenhower's New Look policy with a policy called "flexible response." Flexible response meant that the United States would strengthen its conventional troops while simultaneously expanding the variety and number of nuclear weapons. A military expansion on all levels would allow the United States to meet any threat that might arise.

Kennedy tried to show the American people and the world that he would take a tough stance in international affairs. In his inaugural address he said, "Let every nation know, whether it wishes us well or ill, that we shall pay any price, bear any burden, meet any hardship, support any friend, oppose any foe to assure the survival and the success of liberty."[69] Kennedy also promised to attract the Third World—developing countries in Asia, Africa, and Latin America—to the American side of the Cold War. Fearing the spreading influence of communism, Kennedy spoke often about the need for discipline for the Soviet Union as well as Communist China. Eager to demonstrate his authority in the world, Kennedy prepared for his first meeting with Khrushchev and commented, "I have to show him that we can be as tough as he. I'll have to sit down with him and let him see who he's dealing with."[70] Approaching the relationship with the Soviets as a kind of contest, the Kennedy administration kept regular count of the missiles, rockets, nuclear weapons, and even Third World influence each country had.

President John F. Kennedy addresses the U.S. Congress in 1961. Kennedy's efforts to win the Cold War included increasing the United States' number of nuclear weapons.

THE BERLIN WALL

Despite his hard-line approach toward Khrushchev and the policy of flexible response, Kennedy quickly found that he had no adequate response for the situation that began unfolding in Berlin, deep within the Soviet satellite state of East Germany. In the summer of 1961, increasing numbers of East Germans were using Berlin as an escape route to West Germany. Movement throughout all zones in Berlin was unrestricted; many East Berliners worked in West Berlin and vice versa. Hence, East Germans who wanted to flee could simply travel to Berlin and cross into the Western sector. There they could check into a refugee assembly point that typically screened and interviewed hundreds of refugees daily.

Funded by West Germany, whose cities' economic expansion demanded additional workers, many refugees were flown from Berlin safely to other parts of the country. Lured by the thriving and colorful streets of West Berlin, a showplace of capitalist comforts, people fled the drab, rationed life of the East. There was little the Soviets could do to prevent the exodus. As Khrushchev later put it:

> At a certain stage, ideological issues are decided by the stomach, that is, by seeing who can provide the most for the people's daily needs. Therefore, the attraction of one or the other system is literally decided by the shop windows, by the price of goods, and by wages. In these areas, of course, we had no chance of compet-

ing with the West, especially in West Berlin, where capitalism gave handouts to sharply contrast the material wealth of West Berlin with the living conditions in East Berlin.[71]

To stop the outflow, the Soviets demanded negotiations for ending the Western occupation of Berlin. Rather than addressing the request, however, President Kennedy responded by asking Congress for an additional $3.2 billion in defense funding and the authority to call up military reservists. As East Germans continued to leave through Berlin in increasing numbers, the Soviets decided to take drastic measures. During the night of August 12, East German soldiers closed the Berlin crossing points and began to erect a barbed wire fence between East and West Berlin. Border guards and motorized infantry began stopping all traffic between the two sectors of the city. Within the next few days, the fence was replaced with a massive concrete and barbed wire structure to barricade East Berlin from its Western half. East German border guards were stationed along it and ordered to shoot people who tried to escape to the other side of the Wall.

President Kennedy was outraged. He sent Vice President Lyndon B. Johnson to Berlin to assure the Western sector that it would not be abandoned. Johnson delivered a message guaranteeing West Berlin's freedom and free access to Berlin for

Barbed wire tops the Berlin Wall to stop the flow of East Germans into West Germany. The Wall was torn down in 1989.

Western nations. But during the next few days it was apparent that there was little else the United States could do. The Berlin Wall was left to separate East and West Berlin. Over the next twenty-eight years, many East Germans would be killed trying to cross the barrier to freedom in the West.

While initially the Wall brought some stability to Berlin, it became one of the most striking and hated symbols of the split between the East and West. The imposing physical barricade that separated Berlin was a sobering reminder of the ideological division between East and West, between communism and capitalism, and between the Soviet Union and the United States.

THE CUBAN MISSILE CRISIS

While the Berlin Wall represented Kennedy's first major clash with the Soviets, it was in Latin America, not Europe, where he would face his most terrifying crisis when he took over Eisenhower's plan to invade Cuba

In 1959 rebel leader Fidel Castro succeeded in ousting American ally and dictator Fulgencio Batista to take control of the island nation. Because Eisenhower had tried to install a U.S.-friendly military regime and to prevent Castro's victory, Castro was intensely anti-American.

Determined to undermine American interests in Cuba, Castro spoke out against Americans and began seizing U.S. property in early 1960. At that time, Americans owned over 3 million acres of land in Cuba. American interests controlled about 40 percent of the country's sugar production and 90 percent of its telephone and electric utilities. In addition, the United States and Cuba were active trade partners; about 70 percent of Cuba's imports came from the United States.

In response to Castro's anti-American stance, in mid-1960 Eisenhower decreased the U.S. purchase of Cuban sugar. Sugar was Cuba's main crop, and the international sugar trade brought in the majority of the country's revenues. Thus the reduction in trade with the United States was an immediate blow to Castro's economy. In retaliation, Castro seized American companies on a much larger scale and proclaimed his loyalty to communism. In addition, he appealed to the Soviet Union for aid. The Soviet Union responded with loans and gradually expanded trade with its new communist brother.

Eventually, Eisenhower broke off diplomatic relations with Cuba. And just before he left office, he made plans for an invasion of Cuba. When Kennedy took office, he reviewed the plans and approved the military offensive. According to the invasion plan, Cuban exiles who had been trained under Eisenhower by the CIA would land at the Bay of Pigs in Cuba. After the invaders had secured a beachhead, the Cuban people would rise up against Castro. This dissent would allow the United States to install a military council in Havana to rule the country.

But the expedition did not go as planned. The Cuban exile group departed from Nicaragua on April 6, 1961, but when they reached the Bay of Pigs, they found the Cuban militia waiting for them.

CHECKPOINT CHARLIE

Checkpoint Charlie was the main border crossing point in the Berlin Wall. It was a small, simple building used to control the flow of people between East and West Berlin. Like the Wall itself, Checkpoint Charlie became a symbol of the Cold War rivalry and the strident measures taken to separate East from West.

Checkpoint Charlie was the only crossing point in the Berlin Wall for diplomats and non-Germans. Manned by military guards from the United States, France, and Britain, Checkpoint Charlie gets its name from the U.S. military alphabet. Alpha and Bravo had already been constructed, and Charlie, representing the third station to be built, came next in the military alphabet.

Checkpoint Charlie, along with other parts of the Wall, was also the scene of all kinds of elaborate and spectacular escapes. East Berliners tried to pass through the checkpoint dressed in Soviet uniform, hide in the engines of cars or in potato shipments, or even ride in a hot air balloon over the border. Although many people were killed trying to cross the Wall, many East German border guards, despite instructions, either refused to shoot or deliberately shot to injure rather than kill. Some border guards even aided or participated in escape attempts.

Checkpoint Charlie witnessed exciting and terrifying events in October 1961. American envoy Allan Lightner planned to drive through the checkpoint with his wife to go to the opera, when he was ordered by East German border guards to show his identity papers. This was a violation of agreements in which personnel from all four Allied powers (the United States, France, Britain, and the Soviet Union) were allowed free access throughout Berlin. Lightner refused to produce his papers instigating a larger confrontation. Both U.S. tanks and Soviet tanks approached the area and squared off in a standstill. For several days, the tanks stood facing one other, until Khrushchev recalled the Soviet tanks. As quoted in *Checkpoint Charlie and the Wall: A Divided People Rebel*, Khrushchev offered a simple explanation to his confidantes as to why he backed down in the standoff.

"Every child knows that tanks either move forward or backward. Had the tanks gone forward, it would have meant war, if they went back it meant peace. Berlin had no importance for us, and therefore I ordered our tanks to withdraw."

Following the tearing down of the Wall and the subsequent reunification of Germany, Checkpoint Charlie has become a fascinating part of Cold War history. The area, surrounded by bustling business development, now houses a museum that is a reminder of the hundreds who died trying to escape through the Wall.

AMERICAN INTEREST IN CUBA

In Rise to Globalism, *historian Stephen E. Ambrose explains that America's obsession with Cuba and hatred of Fidel Castro were based on America's growing economic interests in the country. U.S. ownership of sugar mines and plantations in Cuba yielded great profits for American businessmen while prolonging poverty in Cuba.*

"All of America's difficulties in the underdeveloped world came to a head in Cuba. Throughout the nineteenth century, Americans had looked with undisguised longing toward the island. In 1898 they drove the Spanish out and occupied it. After the Cubans wrote a constitution that gave the United States the right to intervene on the island whenever Washington felt it was necessary, the American troops left. Investors stayed behind. Three times after 1902 the United States intervened in Cuba to protect the investments, which by the end of World War II had grown to impressive proportions. Americans owned 80 percent of Cuba's utilities, 40 percent of its sugar, 90 percents of its mining wealth, and occupied the island's key strategic location of Guantanamo Bay. Cuban life was controlled from Washington, for almost the only source of income was sugar, and by manipulating the amount of sugar allowed into the United States, Washington directed the economy. . . . In January, 1959, Fidel Castro, who had placed himself at the head of the various anti-Batista guerrilla movements, drove Batista from power. At first the general public in the United States welcomed Castro, casting him in a romantic mold and applauding his democratic reforms. American supporters of Castro expected him to restore civil liberties, . . . look to the United States for leadership, . . . and not to tamper with the fundamental source of Cuba's poverty, American ownership of the mines and sugar plantations."

Within two days the invasion fell apart completely, and most of the twelve hundred Cuban exiles were captured or killed by Castro's troops.

The Kennedy administration was acutely embarrassed by the Bay of Pigs debacle. More determined then ever to crush Castro's regime, Kennedy and his advisers evaluated their options. Led by the president's brother, Attorney General Robert Kennedy, the administration instructed the CIA to begin Operation Mongoose. As Robert Kennedy put it, the purpose of Operation Mongoose was "to stir things up on the island with espionage, sabotage, [and] general disorder."[72] CIA agents worked to further impair the sugar trade, to oust Cuba from international organizations, and to provide aid to anti-Castro groups based in Miami. Operation Mongoose and the Kennedy administration's obsession with Cuba paved the way for one of the most frightening events of the Cold War.

Displeased by American interference in the affairs of the Soviets' new ally, Khrushchev decided to bulk up his military posture in the area. Pressured by the communist establishment to adopt a more severe approach toward the Americans, and determined to protect the Castro communist regime from a second American invasion, Khrushchev decided to install intermediate and medium-range ballistic missiles in Cuba. Khrushchev claimed, "Our aim was to strengthen and to reinforce Cuba. . . . Any reasonable person has to understand that we never pursued aggressive goals. . . . Our only goal in placing the missiles in Cuba was to prevent any encroachment on Cuban sovereignty and to assure the capability of the Cuban people to be the masters of their own country."[73]

On October 14, 1962, an American U-2 plane photographed Soviet nuclear missile installations on the island within range of

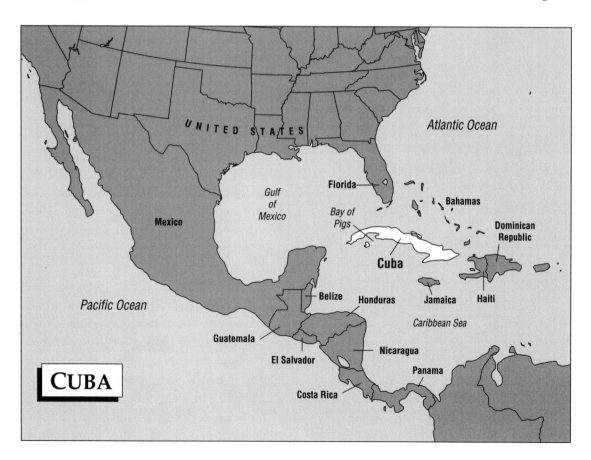

CUBA

targets in the United States. The Kennedy administration was stunned. Rather than discussing the matter with the Soviet Union, Kennedy ordered a special advisory committee to come up with a way to remove the missiles. Secretary of Defense Robert McNamara proposed that the United States impose a naval blockade of Cuba to prevent further military ship-

Communist Fidel Castro became Cuba's leader in 1959. He adopted an anti-American stance and was supported by the Soviet Union.

ments and demand that the current missiles be dismantled and returned to the Soviet Union. American warships headed to the Caribbean waters and the message was sent to Khrushchev demanding removal of the missiles.

As the two countries sent publicized messages back and forth to solve the matter, the world held its breath. For thirteen days it seemed to citizens of both the United States and the Soviet Union that the situation could easily erupt into a nuclear war. In his first communication on the matter, Khrushchev replied that the missiles would be removed if the United States promised to never again invade Cuba. He later added that the United States should also remove American missiles from Turkey, situated on the Soviet border. Kennedy publicly accepted the first demand but seemed to ignore the second.

It is now known, however, that Kennedy did not completely ignore the second request but instead, through his brother Robert, sent a private message to Khrushchev. In it, he promised that the missiles in Turkey would be removed at a future date. On October 28, 1962, Khrushchev accepted the American pledge and removed the missiles from Cuba. The crisis was averted.

Realizing how close they had come to a nuclear conflict, both leaders pledged to work toward better understanding. The crucial messages between the leaders had been slow to travel across the Atlantic Ocean, and the superpowers agreed that improved communication was necessary. A hotline was installed between Moscow and Washington, D.C., that would allow the American and Soviet leaders to be in immediate contact. The two countries also moved to sign a nuclear test ban treaty, and refrained from further confrontations over the situation in Berlin.

The Cuban missile crisis was one of the most frightening moments of the Cold War and human history. Both countries were to blame for provocative behavior. The Soviets were misguided in deciding to install the weapons, and Kennedy was probably mistaken for not negotiating with Khrushchev privately on the matter.

In 1963, the United States removed its missiles from Turkey. U.S. officials claimed the action had no connection to the Cuban missile crisis, but that the missiles were simply outdated and Kennedy wanted them removed.

Viet Minh leader Ho Chi Minh declared Vietnam's independence from Japan in 1945.

THE VIETNAM WAR

In Cuba, the United States and the Soviet Union had faced off in a terrifying crisis. In Vietnam, the two countries would find themselves trapped in an ongoing tragedy. Lasting from the mid-1950s to the mid-1970s, the Vietnam War saw the two sides backing opposing armies in a drawn-out civil war. Five American presidents, from Truman to Nixon, would increase the U.S. presence in the small Southeast Asian country with the same goal: to prevent the victory of communism. Especially devastating to the United States, the Vietnam War proved to be the longest war in U.S. history and a crippling defeat in the Cold War.

The story of imperialism in Vietnam begins with the French, who took over the country in the late nineteenth century. The French authority collapsed, however, during World War II, when the Japanese moved into the area. In 1945, the Viet Minh, an anti-imperialist coalition led by communist Ho Chi Minh, fought the Japanese and declared Vietnam's independence. When World War II ended, the French returned with the intention of retaking control of the country. Truman supported the American ally with financial and material aid. Later, when the French suffered defeat in 1954, the American government was unwilling to see Vietnam fall to communism.

Under President Eisenhower, the U.S. government sent American advisers to

THE DOMINO THEORY

The "domino theory" was used to justify U.S. involvement in Southeast Asia, in particular the war in Vietnam. In essence, according to the "domino theory," if one Pacific nation fell to communism, the momentum would cause the next country to fall, followed by the next, and so on. This chain reaction would be similar to a toppling line of dominoes.

Although the theory clearly has roots in Truman's containment policy, Eisenhower first mentioned dominoes in a press conference on April 7, 1954. Eisenhower used the imagery of dominoes to express his concern that French defeat in Vietnam might ultimately result in a communist triumph throughout Indochina, Burma, and Thailand that would extend to threaten countries such as Australia and New Zealand.

bolster the regime of Ngo Dinh Diem, the leader of South Vietnam who opposed Ho Chi Minh. Unfortunately, Diem was a dictatorial leader, with little local support and many enemies. Diem abolished village elections, threw dissenters into jail, shut down independent newspapers, and repressed Buddhist peasants. Meanwhile, in the North, the Viet Minh gained strength by recruiting many of the peasants that had been victimized by Diem. Communist and other anti-Diem groups joined in a new movement called the National Liberation Front, or Viet Cong. A rebellion, begun as a war against French imperialism, now erupted into civil war between North and South.

When Kennedy entered the White House in 1961, the United States had about three thousand advisers in Vietnam. Kennedy viewed the situation as an international conflict rather than a civil war.

Believing that all communist movements could be traced to the Soviet Union or China, he felt that a communist victory was equal to an American defeat. Humiliated by the events in Berlin and at the Bay of Pigs, JFK desperately wanted a Cold War victory. The young president adhered to the domino theory, which said that the loss of Vietnam to communism would allow other countries to succumb to communism as well. According to his brother Robert, "The President felt that he had a strong, overwhelming reason for being in Vietnam and that we should win the war in Vietnam. . . . If you lost Vietnam, I think everybody was quite clear that the rest of Southeast Asia would fall."[74]

While the North Vietnamese did receive massive support from the Soviet Union and China, in essence the Viet Cong was an independent force. When the North began an armed revolt against Diem in the

South, local communist guerrillas quickly joined the movement. The rebel umbrella group, the National Liberation Front (NLF), enjoyed considerable support among a number of communist and non-communist groups who all opposed Diem's repressive policies. The Soviet Union backed the NLF with material assistance, but it did not send personnel to the region as the United States had done.

Determined to keep South Vietnam from communism, JFK increased U.S. aid to the South Vietnamese government. Soon there were sixteen thousand American advisers in Vietnam. These advisers included Green Beret troops, or coun-

terinsurgency forces specifically trained to beat communist guerrilla forces. By 1963, Kennedy had decided that Diem must be removed because of his ruthless tactics. Through the CIA, the U.S. government encouraged South Vietnamese generals to stage a coup. However, Kennedy was shocked to learn in early November 1963 that Diem had not simply been overthrown; he had been captured and murdered. Only three weeks later, Kennedy himself was assassinated.

After Kennedy's death, the task of containing communism in Vietnam fell to Lyndon B. Johnson. The new president altered the nature of the war by sending

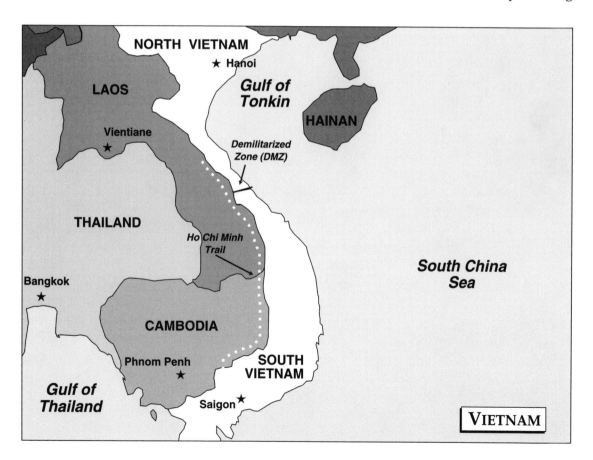

American troops to Vietnam in 1965. He gradually escalated the U.S. involvement. The results were disastrous. Thousands of American soldiers died. In addition, the war caused great dissent back home. Television gave many Americans an up-front look at the brutality of war for the first time, as millions tuned in regularly to the nightly news. Domestic opposition to the war grew dramatically, especially among college students and youth, and the administration lost a great deal of credibility among American citizens.

By the time Richard Nixon assumed the presidency in 1971, the nation was torn apart by dissent. Nixon slowly began to withdraw American troops and transfer the American role to a revamped South Vietnamese army. This army suffered defeated in 1975, which quickly led to South Vietnam's collapse.

The Vietnam War was devastating to the morale of the United States. Debate continues as to why America got involved, why the country accelerated its involvement, and why ultimately it lost. However, most historians agree that the policy of containment was the major factor in bringing the United States into the war. Despite the accelerating catastrophes

Two American soldiers wait for a wave of helicopters to land in the An Lao Valley of South Vietnam.

President Nixon points to a map of Southeast Asia. Nixon withdrew American troops from South Vietnam by 1973.

and loss of human lives, the desire to defeat communism probably served to keep the United States intricately involved. For Kennedy and other presidents, Vietnam seemed to present an opportunity to defeat communism in Asia, but the battle could not be won.

The Vietnam War was, by any measure, a catastrophic conflict. Up to 3 million Vietnamese, Laotians, and Cambodians and over fifty-eight thousand Americans died. Large territories in Vietnam were destroyed, and miles of farmland remained poisoned for many years by chemicals used in the war. In the United States, war veterans suffered crippling physical and mental injuries, and many returned home to be shunned by their fellow Americans for their role in the unpopular war.

The War also had an effect on international politics. The United States was far less willing to involve itself in the Third World. The Soviet Union, on the other hand, seemed more willing to engage in international affairs and began to increase its assistance to struggling Marxists.

Chapter 7

Détente and After

Despite the war that raged on in Vietnam, the United States and the Soviet Union continued to work toward an improved relationship. The Cuban missile crisis had been frightening enough to convince both sides that they needed to steer the world away from the brink of a nuclear holocaust. The result was a new policy, called détente, that was initially effective in improving the relationship between the Soviet Union and the United States. Originating during the Nixon administration, détente, however, seemed to have a different significance for the United States than it did for the Soviet Union. This discrepancy laid the foundation for the détente's demise. By the time that President Ronald Reagan came to office, détente was dead.

THE ROOTS OF DÉTENTE

In the United States, détente was actively pursued by Republican president Richard M. Nixon. Arriving in the White House in January 1969, Nixon turned from his previously strict anticommunist stance in favor of improved mutual understanding. At his inauguration, Nixon declared:

By the time Nixon became president, his anticommunist stance had changed to one of understanding and negotiation.

"After a period of confrontation, we are entering an era of negotiation. Let all nations know that during this administration, the lines of communication will be open. We cannot expect to make everyone our friend, but we can try to make no one our enemy.... The peace we seek and the peace we seek to win is not victory over another people, but the peace that comes with healing in its wings;... with understanding for those that have opposed us.[75]"

Nixon's foreign policy agenda was shaped strongly by the input of Henry Kissinger. Kissinger served as Nixon's national security adviser until 1973 and then secretary of state. Kissinger, a German-born political scientist, pursued a foreign policy based on restraint and limited cooperation through negotiation. Kissinger's view of world politics emphasized that five, not two, superpowers— the United States, the Soviet Union, China, Western Europe, and Japan—must work together to solve the world's problems and preserve order. These powerful entities should be taking each other's interests into consideration and learn to negotiate and cooperate. Kissinger believed that rather than trying to change the Soviet approach to world politics, the United States should seek to cooperate with the USSR. This policy was especially attractive to the American public after the Cuban missile crisis and the disastrous American involvement in Vietnam.

Soviet leaders also sought to establish a more stable relationship with the United States during the era of détente. Leonid Brezhnev, who had deposed Nikita Khrushchev in 1964, was highly focused on foreign affairs. After pursuing a massive military buildup that entailed expanding nuclear and conventional power, by the late 1960s Brezhnev proudly saw the Soviet Union on level footing with the United States. Now that the Soviet Union and the United States were military equals, the time was ripe for cooperation. According to Brezhnev, "In the new situation, the leaders of the bourgeois world have also come to realize that the Cold War has outlived itself and that there is need for a new, sensible, and realistic policy. Our calls for peaceful coexistence have begun to evoke serious responses in many capitalist countries."[76] In addition, like the Americans, the Soviets feared a continually spiraling nuclear arms race that would be both dangerous and expensive. Brezhnev also realized that expanded trade with the United States would greatly help the Soviet economy, which had been severely damaged by the

Secretary of State Henry Kissinger's foreign policy emphasized unity among the world's superpowers.

cost of the military buildup. The Soviets needed technology and other goods from the U.S. in order to improve their standard of living.

DÉTENTE HIGHLIGHTS: CHINA, SALT I, AND THE HELSINKI ACCORDS

Détente did not refer only to the relationship between the United States and the Soviet Union. Nixon and Kissinger also sought to improve their relationship with another communist rival, the People's Republic of China. Although the United States had refused to recognize Mao's PRC in 1949, and although it had fought against China in the Korean War, Nixon now forged a friendlier relationship. He did this for several reasons. First, he hoped that opening Chinese markets to American exports would boost the U.S. economy. In addition, because the Soviet Union and the PRC had become rivals in the 1960s, the United States and the PRC now shared a common fear: the rise of Soviet military power. Nixon strategized that a normalized relationship with China would create a balance of power that would put pressure on the Soviet giant.

With these goals in mind, Nixon and Kissinger traveled to China in February 1972. The trip was historic, as no American president had ever visited China. China's foreign minister, Zhou Enlai, greeted Kissinger at the airport with the words, "Ah, old friend."[77] President Nixon, at a state dinner one evening, recited a poem written by his host, Communist Party chairman Mao Zedong. A raving success, the trip was instrumental in opening up a fresh dialogue with China that has continued to this day. It also set the stage for the United States to extend official diplomatic recognition to the PRC a few years later, in 1979.

Nixon's strategy of putting pressure on the Soviets through improved relations with China was successful. Shortly after he returned to America, Moscow indicated that it was ready to discuss the issue of limiting nuclear arms. In May, Nixon headed to Moscow, where he and Brezhnev

Soviet president Leonid Brezhnev in Paris. Brezhnev greatly favored cooperation between the Soviet Union and the United States.

被压迫民族联合起来！

President Nixon (right) inspects a Chinese honor guard with President Zhou Enlai (center).

worked out the first ever arms agreement between their two countries. Coming on the heels of the successful trip to China, the new agreements were stunning. For the first time in decades, the United States had forged a mutual understanding with both communist giants. Nixon explained this new world in a speech to Congress upon his return, proclaiming:

> For decades, America has been locked in hostile confrontation with two great Communist powers, the Soviet Union and the People's Republic of China. . . . Our relationships with both had reached a deadly impasse. . . . But now in the brief space of four months, these journeys to Peking and to Moscow have begun to free us from perpetual confrontation. We have moved toward better understanding, mutual respect, and point-by-point settlement of differences with both the major Communist powers. . . . The threat of war has not been eliminated—it has been reduced. We are making progress toward a world in which leaders of nations will settle their differences by negotiation, not by force, and in which they learn to live with their differences so that their sons will not have to die for those differences.[78]

The arms agreement signed in Moscow was called the Strategic Arms Limitation Treaty, or SALT I. In the first part of the treaty, the United States and the USSR agreed to limit their antiballistic missile systems (ABMs), weapons used to intercept offensive missiles. Historically, as one country increased its number of ABMs, the other would manufacture more and more offensive missiles to overcome ABM protection. The idea, therefore, was that limiting ABMs would slow down the spiraling arms race. In the second part of SALT I, the two countries placed a five-year moratorium on the number of offensive nuclear missiles each side could have in inventory. This provision was flawed because it imposed constraints only on the number of missiles each country could have, yet it placed no restrictions on the number of nuclear warheads—the element that makes a missile a formidable weapon. Nonetheless, SALT I was important because it was the first ever agreement between the two countries to put limitations on the nuclear arms race.

There were other positive aspects of détente. In the Quadripartite Berlin Agreement of 1971, Russia formally agreed to guarantee France, Great Britain, and the United States access to West Berlin. In addition, U.S.-Soviet trade tripled in 1971 and 1972. When the Soviets suffered a poor grain harvest in 1972, they struck a deal with the United States whereby American grain worth $1 billion was sold to the Soviets at very attractive prices. (While the deal helped the Soviets and increased trade between the nations, some Americans complained when grain prices at home rose due to decreased supply.)

The high point of détente came in Helsinki, Finland, in 1974, when representaties from about 35 countries met for the Conference on Security and Cooperation in Europe. The Western powers formally accepted the Soviet border changes that had taken place at the end of World War II, recognition the Soviets had sought for over thirty years. Known as the Helsinki Accords, the agreements also encouraged trade and scientific cooperation among countries and guaranteed human rights and the free movement of people and ideas. As Brezhnev and President Gerald Ford, who had replaced Nixon after he was forced to resign, met in Helsinki to sign the accords, 140 miles above earth the American *Apollo* spacecraft docked with its Soviet counterpart, *Soyuz*. U.S.-Soviet cooperation seemed at an all-time high.

DÉTENTE'S DEMISE: CARTER'S HUMAN RIGHTS AGENDA AND SOVIETS IN AFGHANISTAN

Once President Jimmy Carter entered the White House in 1977, however, it became apparent that the glow of U.S.- Soviet cooperation would be short-lived. Carter promised to reduce the number of American troops overseas, and to cut back in the nuclear arms race. He pledged to continue détente but the "soul of our foreign policy," he said, would be human rights. Carter called for "a new foreign policy—a policy based on constant decency in its values and on optimism in the nation's historical mission."[79] Carter aimed to replace the negative and simple focus of anticommunism with a more positive policy that Americans could be proud of—the

PRAGUE SPRING

In 1968, Czechoslovakia experienced a brief period of democratic reforms, known as the Prague Spring, under leader Alexander Dubček. Dubček's goal was to reform Soviet-style Marxist-Leninism into a more democratic form of socialism. He hoped to reform the economy that had been suffering from overproducing heavy industrial goods while neglecting other pursuits. In addition, he began to relax censorship on the press, and debate within the country flourished. He called his idea "socialism with a human face." Dubček's work was strongly supported by Czechoslovak citizens, who had participated in a democratic government between World War I and World War II.

However, the Soviets began to fear that the Czechoslovak Communist Party might lose power or that Dubček might change sides in the Cold War. The Prague Spring came to an end when Soviet-led Warsaw Pact troops entered the country in August 1968. Dubček and other reform leaders were arrested and demonstrations were crushed.

After squelching the Prague Spring, Leonid Brezhnev made a speech in which he discussed the Prague situation and indicated that the Soviet Union would intervene, if necessary, in socialist countries to save socialism in the name of strengthening the socialist community. A justification for intervention abroad, the policy became known as the Brezhnev doctrine. The Brezhnev doctrine would be used in the future to secure socialism and the Soviet Union's power over its satellites. It remained in force until 1989, when Mikhail Gorbachev denounced the policy.

Czechoslovakian youths protest Soviet invaders in Prague, in 1968.

championship of human rights. These included the freedom to work, to worship, to vote, to travel, and to receive a fair trial.

Despite Carter's good intentions, détente deteriorated during his administration. Although détente's decline cannot be fully blamed on the Carter administration, the president's focus on human rights, often ill-timed, grew increasingly irksome to the Soviets. In 1977, for example, Carter strongly criticized the treatment of human rights activists in the Soviet Union just before sending Brezh-

President Jimmy Carter tried to shift the focus of U.S. foreign policy from anticommunism to human rights.

nev a new arms control proposal. Soviet foreign minister Andrei Gromyko expressed irritation, saying, "We do not need any teachers when it comes to the internal affairs of our country."[80]

Détente's demise was most likely due to the fact that the Soviet Union and the United States had differing views of what détente actually entailed. For the United States, détente meant that the Soviets had agreed to show restraint in spreading communism to other parts of the world. The Soviets, on the other hand, viewed détente's cooperation as limited strictly to specific agreements and negotiations. While it was in their interest to cooperate on many issues, they believed that their improved military strength and global political standing now meant that gave them license to support Marxist regimes without the interference and condemnation of the United States.

Thus, when in 1975, the Soviets assisted a Marxist faction to win a civil war in Angola, the United States was both shocked and angry. The fact that the Soviets flew Cuban troops to Africa to help the Marxists win the battle further enraged American policy makers. Soviet-sponsored Cuban troops also helped to support a Marxist dictatorship in Ethiopia in 1977. The United States began to view the Soviet Union with renewed suspicion.

When the Soviets invaded Afghanistan in 1979, it was final proof that America and the Soviet Union had dramatically divergent views of détente. In 1978, procommunist revolutionaries had overthrown the Afghanistan government and established a new Afghan communist regime. Although

A Soviet tank rolls through a street during the Afghan civil war in 1979.

communist rule was very unpopular in this Islamic country, in December 1979 the Soviet Red Army invaded Afghanistan to install a new communist leadership. The initial invasion was successful, but local Afghan troops fought back with determination. Soon, the Soviet Union was embroiled in a drawn-out guerrilla war that many likened to the U.S. involvement in Vietnam.

Carter, highly displeased with the Soviet aggression in Afghanistan, decided to discipline the Soviets. Having signed SALT II agreements with Brezhnev in June, Carter now withdrew SALT II from the Senate ratification process. He also suspended grain and technology shipments to Russia, and launched an international boycott of the 1980 Olympics that were to take place in Moscow. Although he had entered the White House with hopes of ending the Cold War, by the time Carter left office in 1980, Soviet-American relations seemed to be at an all-time low.

THE END OF DÉTENTE: RONALD REAGAN AND THE EVIL EMPIRE

When Ronald Reagan came into the White House, it was clear that détente was dead. A fervent anticommunist since the 1950s, Reagan was critical that détente policies had allowed the Soviet nuclear arms

THE IRAN HOSTAGE CRISIS

Jimmy Carter's ability to deal with the Soviets was severely impaired in the last year of his presidency by the critical situation in Iran. In early 1979, the shah of Iran had been ousted by revolutionaries under the leadership of the Ayatollah Ruhollah Khomeini, an anti-American Muslim cleric. The United States had a long-standing relationship with the shah, as the CIA restored him to the throne in 1953 by overturning the democratically elected communist-leaning Mossadegh government. The CIA had also trained and aided the shah's secret police force.

In November 1979 U.S. officials allowed the shah into the United States, ostensibly for medical treatment but effectively offering him asylum. Khomeini was furious. His military followers stormed the American embassy in Tehran, taking fifty-two Americans as hostages. He demanded the return of the shah for trial in Iran.

Carter refused to return the shah or to apologize for American involvement in Iran. He attempted to secure the release of the hostages through public appeals and economic pressure, and he ordered that Iranian assets in the United States be frozen. Nothing worked. In April 1980, Carter broke off diplomatic relations with Iran, and ordered a risky rescue mission. His plan failed and eight American soldiers were killed.

The botched mission further impaired the Carter presidency, and Carter continued to fail in his appeals for the freedom of the hostages. The American hostages finally gained their freedom in January 1981, 444 days after their capture and shortly after the new American president Ronald Reagan entered the White House.

Iranian captors parade their American hostages, who were held for 444 days.

President Reagan opposed détente and greatly increased the United States' arms budget.

Americans and verbally attack the USSR. He asked "Would the Soviets ever use their formidable military power? Well, again, can we afford to believe they won't?"[81] The president criticized and debased the Soviets, claiming, "The only morality they recognize is that which will further their cause, meaning they reserve unto themselves the right to commit any crime, to lie, to cheat, in order to attain that."[82] Reagan's secretary of state, Alexander Haig, supported the notion of the Soviet military threat and warned the Soviets that peace was not a priority of the new administration, saying, "There are more important things than peace . . . there are things which we Americans must be willing to fight for."[83]

Meanwhile Brezhnev's health was deteriorating, and he died in November 1982. His position went uncontested to Yuri Andropov, former head of the KGB. Although Western leaders expected hard-nosed conservatism from a former KGB leader, Andropov's first few months were marked by a "peace offensive." He repeatedly called for arms reduction and a new U.S.-Soviet summit. He proposed nuclear-free zones for parts of Europe and the Mediterranean and a ban on arms sales to developing nations. In the 1983 Warsaw Pact meeting, Andropov suggested a nonaggression policy for both NATO and the Warsaw Pact in which all members would agree not to use force against any other member.

But Reagan was unreceptive to these ideas. Only days after Andropov's appeal for nonaggression among Warsaw Pact and NATO members, Reagan gave a speech in which he called the Soviet Union an evil

buildup to surpass that of the United States. Believing that Soviet military power was a threat to America, Reagan undertook the largest peacetime military buildup in the country's history. One of his first proposals was a five-year, $1.7 trillion defense budget. In a televised address on March 23, 1983, Reagan emphasized the Soviet threat to the United States in an attempt to gain public support for further military expenditures. He spoke of the Soviets' massive stockpile of nuclear weapons and warned that the Soviets could easily strike directly at the United States.

Reagan's use of unsettling Cold War rhetoric seemed aimed to both scare empire. A few weeks later, he began to push for a new nuclear arms project called the Strategic Defense Initiative, or SDI.

The project was designed to use new, still unproven, technology in outer space to defend against nuclear attack. From the start, SDI was controversial. Critics remarked that the technology, if it were even success- ful, would be vastly expensive. Others said SDI violated ABM agreements that the Americans had signed with the Soviets in 1972. The Soviets also spoke out strongly against SDI. Andropov called the project "not just irresponsible. It is insane."[84]

Reagan's clearest divergence from dé- tente policies was in his approach to devel-

KAL Flight 007

Mystery still surrounds the events of August 31, 1983, when a South Korean airliner, KAL Flight 007, was shot down in Soviet airspace, killing all 269 people aboard, including 61 Americans. Jeremy Isaacs and Taylor Downing, in Cold War: An Illustrated History, 1945–1991, *summarizes the questions the event prompted:*

"KAL 007 was on a regular flight from New York to Seoul. It stopped to refuel at Anchorage where, unusually, it took on more fuel than it needed before continuing its journey. From there, Captain Chun Byung-in, a veteran of the Korean war and one of the airline's most experienced pilots, flew the aircraft on a route that from the start be- gan to drift off course. . . . There are still unanswered questions about what happened. Was the flight off course due to some extra- ordinary coincidence of navigational accidents? Had the Soviets jammed its navigation system for some reason? Was Captain Chun deliberately trying to take a short cut to reduce fuel costs? If so, why was he not extra vigilant as he knowingly crossed Soviet airspace? Why, above all else, did KAL Flight 007 not respond to international warning signals from the Soviet fighter, the waggling of wings and then the firing of tracers across its bow? The Soviet pilot has said that he had identified the plane as a Boeing 747 civilian jet, so why then was the order given to shoot it down?

The Soviets alleged that KAL 007 was on a spy mission to pro- voke the Soviet defenses in a way that could then be observed by US electronic surveillance systems. This has never been proved. Nine years after the incident, a Russian investigation concluded that the shoot-down was a genuine accident by panicky and incompetent Soviet Air Defense Command operator.

In any case, at a particularly tense moment in the Cold War, the tragic loss of KAL Flight 007 made each side even more suspicious of the other. Reagan exploited the anti-Soviet sentiment generated in the United States to win support for his increased military spending."

American marines march down a street in Greenville during the U.S. invasion of Grenada in 1983.

oping countries, an approach that became known as the Reagan Doctrine. In essence the Reagan Doctrine declared that the United States would use military force and other means to undermine Marxist regimes in the Third World. It was based on the notion that direct military, economic, and political pressure against communist and Marxist movements would put a major strain on the Soviet military and economy. The United States used the Reagan Doctrine as a kind of warning to the Soviets, and quickly showed them that they were willing to back the words. In Afghanistan, for example, the United States supplied weapons to Muslim rebels while the USSR was actively funding and fighting on the other side. Under the Reagan Doctrine, aid was also given to countries fighting Marxism in Latin and South America, which again fueled animosity in the Soviet Union.

In October 1983, Reagan sent marines to the small Caribbean country of Grenada to overthrow a radical Marxist regime. The program was successful. In Nicaragua, where the Soviet Union and

Cuba backed a dictatorial Marxist regime known as Sandinistas, the United States armed the anti-Sandinista forces, known as the Contras. Despite continued U.S. military and economic pressure, Reagan could not bring down the Sandinistas. Eventually, they agreed to free elections in Nicaragua in 1990, and were defeated. In nearby El Salvador, America funded the right-wing military dictatorship in a guerrilla war against leftist fighters funded by Cuba. Trying to keep the nation free from communism, Reagan increased the aid to El Salvador's military dictatorship from $36 million in 1981 to $197 million in 1984.

As proof that the U.S.-Soviet relationship had deteriorated completely, the Soviets walked out of three different sets of arms negotiations. For the first time in twenty years the two countries were not even discussing how to limit the arms race. The Cold War, it seemed, had been fully revived. Andrei Gromyko stated in September 1983, "The world situation is now slipping towards a very dangerous precipice. Problem number one is to avoid a nuclear war."[85]

Chapter

8 The Cold War Comes to a Close

When Mikhail Gorbachev came to power in 1985, Soviet society began to change radically. The new Soviet leader called for greater openness in society and a sweeping restructuring of the economy. In addition, the Soviet Union's relationship with the United States warmed considerably. However, Gorbachev unknowingly unleashed forces within his country that ultimately led to the dismantling of the Eastern bloc in 1989 and to the demise of the USSR in 1991. These events marked a dramatic end of the Cold War and the start of a new era.

GORBACHEV AND GLASNOST

After the deaths of Andropov and his successor, Konstantin Chernenko, the Soviet Communist Party leadership went to Mikhail Gorbachev in March 1985. Gorbachev, a fifty-four-year-old reformer, had introduced the need for greater openness and restructuring in a Party speech the year before. The new leader saw that the Soviet system was riddled with problems. Economically, the country was stagnating. Central planning had proved increasingly inefficient, and new technology lagged far behind that of the rest of the world. Polit-

President Reagan (left) and Mikhail Gorbachev attend a summit together in Iceland in October, 1986.

ically, the Soviet bureaucracy was riddled with corruption. Party leaders enjoyed all kinds of kickbacks and bonuses. Social ills, such as alcoholism, were growing more serious. In addition, defense expenditures had crippled the Soviet budget, making it impossible to deal with these domestic problems effectively.

In an attempt to rejuvenate Soviet society, Gorbachev launched radical reform programs called glasnost and perestroika. Glasnost aimed to liberalize Soviet society, and perestroika called for its economic restructuring. Reflected in these programs were Gorbachev's beliefs that only relaxed controls on information and decreased censorship would lead the way toward economic revitalization. He declared that "profound transformations must be carried out in the economy and the entire system of social relations, and a qualitatively higher standard of living must be ensured for the Soviet people. . . . Glasnost is an integral part of a socialist democracy. Frank information is evidence of confidence in the people and respect for their intelligence, and for their ability to understand events for themselves."[86]

From the start, it was evident that Gorbachev was different from former Soviet leaders. Unlike Brezhnev, for example, who was rarely seen in public, Gorbachev often visited factories or colleges or stopped on the street to chat with ordinary citizens. In addition, his view of international politics demonstrated a need for the Soviet Union to cooperate rather than compete. According to Cold War historians Jeremy Isaacs and Taylor Downing, "Mikhail Gorbachev was from a generation different from that of his predecessors, with attitudes formed not by privations and suffering during the Second World War but by coming of age in a world of coexistence."[87]

Within a year of taking charge, Gorbachev launched a program to tighten discipline and attack corruption within the government. Gorbachev also realized that the Soviet Union could not both compete in an arms race and solve its domestic problems. He understood that funds would have to be reallocated from defense spending to other programs. With this goal in mind, he aggressively pursued plans to stop the arms race. In countless speeches, Gorbachev delivered to the world the message that he was committed to arms reduction. Compromise and cooperation, not confrontation, were needed to move forward, not only in U.S.- Soviet relations but elsewhere in the world. Gorbachev greatly impressed Western nations when he made promises that all troops would be withdrawn from the bloody and drawn-out conflict in Afghanistan. These measures helped to change the viewpoint of Ronald Reagan, who, despite his former stance on the Soviet Union, now accepted Gorbachev's calls for discussion and warmer relations.

REAGAN AND GORBACHEV MEET

The two leaders met in Geneva, Switzerland, on November 19, 1985. While Gorbachev's main agenda was to get Reagan to agree to stop the arms race, Reagan remained firm that the United States would continue to develop SDI. Later, speaking to his aides about the meeting, Gorbachev called Reagan "a political dinosaur."[88] But the next day, the tone of the dialogue changed. The two men spent hours discussing various issues, and seemed to get along well. Although they remained divided by SDI, the summit was viewed as a great success because the two adversaries had established a useful dialogue.

Gorbachev and Reagan met again in Reykjavik, Iceland, in October 1986, and then in Washington, D.C., in December 1987, where the two signed the Intermediate Nuclear Forces (INF) Treaty. The treaty was historic because it eliminated all intermediate-range nuclear arms held by the United States and Soviets in both Eastern and Western Europe. The two countries would no longer have nuclear missiles pointed at one another in Europe. And for the first time, inspection teams from both countries were allowed access to missile sites and the plants where missiles were being dismantled.

At the UN General Assembly meetings in December 1988, Gorbachev applied more heat to the melting Cold War. He spoke of freedom of choice in international relations and seemed to be sending a signal to the countries of Eastern Europe that the Soviet Union would tolerate greater political freedom. Probably realizing that the Soviet budget could no longer afford to prop up Eastern Europe, Gorbachev indicated that Moscow would no longer use military force in the international sphere. His message rang clear: East European countries could choose their own form of government. He declared: "Force or the threat of force neither can nor should be instruments of foreign policy. . . . The principle of the freedom of choice is mandatory. . . . To deny a nation the freedom of choice, regardless of pretext or the verbal guise in which it is cloaked, is to upset the unstable balance that has been achieved. . . . Freedom of choices is a universal principle. It knows no exceptions."[89] Then in a move that stunned the world, Gorbachev an-nounced the unilateral removal of 500,000 Soviet troops, 10,000 tanks, 8,500 pieces of artillery, and 500 combat aircraft from Eastern Europe. This shift provided a catalyst for momentous events to take place in 1989.

REVOLUTIONS IN EASTERN EUROPE

The sweeping reforms Gorbachev implemented in the Soviet Union weakened the resolve of communist leaders in the countries of Eastern Europe, countries that had been under the Soviet grip for over forty years. Communism, mostly inefficient and unpopular in Eastern Europe, began to buckle as citizens called for change.

After a rocky start to the year, in which eight hundred people were arrested during peaceful demonstrations in Prague, 1989 was a year of democratic revolutions throughout Eastern Europe. In January the Hungarian parliament voted to allow freedom of association and to permit the establishment of political parties. Open multiparty elections were scheduled for the following year. In May, Hungarian soldiers began to pull down barbed wire fences between Hungary and Austria, "opening the first chink in the Iron Curtain."[90] In Poland, the communists opened roundtable talks with the Solidarity trade union, a group representing Polish workers and agitating for reform. After discussing the situation for several months, the roundtable participants agreed to hold open elections in June. In the elections, Solidarity won 99 of 100 Senate seats as

Romanians attend a 1989 demonstration for peace in Bucharest, Romania.

well as a majority of seats in the lower house. The communists had been swiftly defeated in Poland.

When Hungary opened its borders with East Germany, it was clear that things were changing radically. Hungary had signed a treaty with East Germany in 1968 agreeing not to allow East Germans to leave for the West through its territory. Now, Hungarian foreign minister Gyal Horn asked the Soviet Union for permission to open Hungary's border; Moscow responded that it had no objections. Horn said, "It was quite obvious to me that this would be the first step in a landslide-like series of events."[91] Despite objections from the East German government, the border was opened. Thirteen thousand East Germans fled to Hungary within the first three days.

In October Gorbachev traveled to Berlin to celebrate East Germany's fortieth anniversary, where he was met by throngs of young communists chanting, "Gorby, save us!"[92] In a speech to the crowds, Gorbachev called for East German leader and Communist Party chief Erich Honecker to introduce Soviet-type reforms. The Soviet leader's visit was followed with protests against the deeply unpopular communist regime as seventy thousand protestors demanding change marched through the city of Leipzig.

But Honecker would not listen to Gorbachev's advice, instead choosing to exercise his military muscle. Honecker ordered his secret police to fire on the dissenters. Angered by the use of force, a group in the East German Politburo decided it was time for Honecker to go.

LECH WALESA

Lech Walesa grabbed international attention in 1980 as the leader of Solidarity, communist Poland's first independent labor union. Born in 1943 in Popowo, Poland, Walesa was the son of a carpenter. He became an electrical engineer in Lenin Shipyard in Gdansk, Poland, in 1967. A strong political activist, Walesa participated in mass demonstrations against rising food prices in 1970 at the shipyard, and was later fired because of his protests. Walesa was arrested many times between 1976 and 1980 for his dissident activities.

Walesa's role in dealing with the communists for greater political freedoms won him international recognition and Western praise. When in July 1980 more than one hundred thousand workers went on strike against rising food prices, the Gdansk shipyards were at the center of the protest. On August 14, 1980, workers seized control of the shipyard. Walesa, quickly named their leader, met with Poland's first deputy premier to negotiate an agreement to give workers the right to organize freely and independently. In September, Walesa organized Solidarity and was elected its chair. The following year, however, the Polish regime cracked down, disbanding Solidarity and arresting Walesa.

Released in 1982, Walesa went on to win the Nobel Peace Prize in 1983, much to the embarrassment of the Polish government. He continued to agitate for reform, and by December 1988 it was becoming clear that increasing numbers of Poles would no longer tolerate the poor economic conditions. In a remarkable move, at the plenary session of the Communist Party, Party leaders invited the illegal and oppositionist Solidarity movement to join in roundtable talks to take place in February 1989. These talks lasted for fifty-nine days. As a result, Solidarity became a legal movement and political reforms were put into place to increase the parliament and to allow Solidarity to nominate candidates. Walesa and his fellow activists began campaigning with enthusiasm.

After elections in June 1989, Solidarity captured ninety-nine of one hundred seats in the Senate and a majority of the lower house as well. Walesa did not run for office himself but actively participated in the new government. In 1989, Walesa ran for the presidency and won by a landslide. As president he led the country through economic and democratic reforms including privatization and Poland's first fully free parliamentary elections in 1991. Walesa lost his reelection campaign in 1995 to Alexander Kwasniewski, the head of the Democratic Left Alliance. Walesa still remains active in Polish politics.

Honecker was ousted and replaced by Egon Krenz, the chief of internal security.

Krenz was young and progressive. He released prisoners from jail and called for "change and removal."[93] Later, he fired the entire cabinet and two-thirds of the Politburo, and opened the borders with Czechoslovakia. When unrest continued he turned to Gorbachev for advice. Gorbachev advised him that all of East Germany's borders would need to be opened in order to restore peace within the country. Thus, on November 9, 1989, the Berlin Wall was opened, allowing East Germans to freely pass into West Berlin. Germans on both sides of the Wall helped to tear it down while singing and celebrating through the night. The Wall, which had separated East and West for twenty-eight years, had finally come down.

The Bulgarian regime fell the next day. The next month, in Prague, Czechoslovakia, a bloodless "Velvet Revolution" forced the Communist Party from power and opened the nation's border to the West. But in Romania, change came violently. Almost one thousand people were killed in the streets of Bucharest in a clash between protestors and local communist forces. Trying to flee the chaos, Romania's communist dictator, Nicolae Ceausescu, and his wife were captured, tried, and executed on Christmas Day. In this dramatic scene, communist control in Eastern Europe had disintegrated. The Cold War itself was nearly over.

A determined man on the Berlin Wall helps another man climb to the other side of it.

A flag is waved over citizens of Prague, Czechoslovakia who are protesting the communist regime in their country.

The official end of the Cold War came in 1990. In a June summit between the United States and the Soviet Union, new U.S. president George Bush and Gorbachev signed agreements dealing with chemical and nuclear weapons. Gorbachev accepted German reunification and the country's entrance into NATO. Germany officially reunified on October 3. In November, the United States, the Soviet Union, and thirty other nations met to sign the Charter of Paris, another official document that served to end the Cold War. The charter included a nonaggression pact between NATO and the Warsaw Pact. Bush said of the meeting, "We have closed a chapter in history. The Cold War is over."[94]

Without a doubt, Gorbachev had been a driving force behind these historic developments. Pushing for reform in Eastern Europe, he unwittingly allowed democratic forces to rise up and overpower communism. A believer in socialism, he did not strive for the failure of communism in Eastern Europe, but once the systems began to crumble, he did nothing to force them back under Soviet control. The only way to save communism in Eastern Europe, he realized, would be with force and most likely bloodshed. Gorbachev understood that cracking down on dissent would have drastic consequences, including the end to his reforms at home. What he did not understand was that his reforms at home had ushered in their own forces for change. Once again, these forces could not be easily reversed.

While the countries of Eastern Europe were busy rejecting communism, Mikhail

Gorbachev found his communist authority challenged from within as well. In February 1990, in a massive demonstration in Moscow, citizens demanded an end to the Communist Party monopoly. Gorbachev responded by proposing a new multiparty system, thereby appeasing the reformers without alienating communist conservatives. Gorbachev was walking a delicate line. In March 1990, Lithuania declared its independence from the USSR. Gorbachev called the move illegitimate and invalid, but he did not use force to stop it. Instead he instituted an economic embargo. One month later, however, Lithuania's fellow Baltic republics of Estonia and Latvia were also calling for independence.

In May 1990 Boris Yeltsin began his rise to power. On May 29 he was chosen by the parliament as the leader of the Russian Republic. Yeltsin was ambitious and popular among the Russian people. He resigned completely from the Communist Party and began to advocate real political change and economic reform. Over the next several months, six republics declared sovereignty. Russia and Ukraine both declared their laws would take precedence over Soviet laws. As the republics asserted their political power, the relationship between the republics and Moscow grew tense. According to historians Isaacs and Downing, "A fork in the road had come clearly into view: one branch pointed toward Gorbachev and a restructured Soviet Union; the other towards Yeltsin and Russia, and the dissolution of the Soviet Union."[95]

Latvians climb onto a fallen statue of Lenin to demonstrate their opposition to communism.

As 1990 came to a close, the Soviet Union under Gorbachev's control had taken major steps to implement reform. The Supreme Soviet had voted to create a multiparty system and to allow freedom of religion. But by the end of the year, Gorbachev, facing pressure from communist hard-liners, changed his strategy and began bringing old guard conservatives back into the government. Soviet foreign minister Eduard Shevardnadze resigned in December, warning that authoritarian forces were overtaking the Soviet government.

Indeed, Soviet tactics had changed. In January 1991, Soviet troops and riot police seized state-owned buildings in Vilnius, Lithuania, and Riga, Latvia. Sunday, January 13 became known as "Bloody Sunday" as Soviet troops stormed the television tower and other buildings in Vilnius, the capital, killing fourteen people. The following Sunday, Soviet forces attacked the Interior Ministry in Riga, killing five Latvians. In Moscow, Gorbachev's stance was unclear. First he defended the actions, later he condemned them. Thousands took to the streets to protest the crackdown.

Gorbachev was struggling to preserve the Soviet Union, and he proposed new ideas to keep the country intact while allowing the republics more autonomy. His Union Treaty, which entailed loosened ties between the republics and the central Soviet government, was approved in a nationwide referendum, but Yeltsin and several republics boycotted the vote. The

A FAREWELL KISS

Mikhail Gorbachev visited Berlin in October 1989, only days before the East German leadership decided to acquiesce to demands to open the Berlin Wall. In the following excerpt from Lenin's Tomb: The Last Days of the Soviet Empire, *David Remnick gives Gorbachev credit for helping to spark events that brought down the Wall.*

"The Berlin visit was one of Gorbachev's finest moments, the sort of subtle exchange that he was made for. A year later, when blunt decisiveness was needed at home, when democratic politics demanded an end to backroom maneuvering, Gorbachev would hesitate and fail. Boris Yeltsin would fill the vacuum. But Gorbachev was the man for this moment. In public, he played along nicely with the East German leadership. In his own speeches and comments, he never drifted far from his host. He kissed Herr Honecker firm on the lips. But in the end that kiss was the kiss of farewell. In private, Gorbachev hinted broadly that the leadership could either begin its own massive reforms or end up defeated and defunct. Gorbachev trotted out one of his favorite aphorisms for the occasion: 'Life itself punishes those who delay.'. . . Such hints can spark a revolution."

Boris Yeltsin was the first democratically elected leader in Russia's history.

without him. In a surprise coup, twelve hard-liners declared themselves the State Committee for the State of Emergency and told the country that Gorbachev was too ill to perform his duties. Gorbachev was placed under house arrest in Foros with all telephones and other means of communication cut off. Conservative vice president Gennadi Yanayev assumed the presidency.

But many in the Soviet government, the army, and the KGB refused to obey the orders of the Emergency Committee. Yeltsin led the resistance from the seat of the Russian parliament, a building in Moscow called the White House. Despite the tensions between the rising Russian republic and the central government, Yeltsin supported Gorbachev as the legitimate Soviet leader. In a historic and courageous appeal to citizens that was read over independent radio and sent through Western wire services, Yeltsin denounced the coup and its plotters and demanded that Gorbachev be released. Yeltsin declared,

situation seemed to be further disintegrating when Georgia declared its independence in April 1991. Two months later, Russians elected Boris Yeltsin to the new post of president of Russia. Yeltsin was now the first democratically elected leader in Russian history.

Meanwhile, Soviet hard-liners in Moscow had been pushing Gorbachev to impose emergency rule. Gorbachev had ignored their requests. In August, after Gorbachev traveled to his vacation home at Foros on the Black Sea, the old-guard communists decided to impose emergency rule

Undoubtedly it is essential to give the country's president, Gorbachev, an opportunity to address the people. Today he has been blockaded. I have been denied communications with him. . . . We are absolutely confident that our countrymen will not permit the sanctioning of the tyranny and lawlessness of the putschists [plotters], who have lost all shame and conscience. We address an appeal to servicemen to manifest lofty civic duty and not take part in the reactionary coup. Until these demands are met, we appeal for a universal unlimited strike.[96]

Yeltsin's supporters flooded the streets around the White House, the building that housed the Russian government, in Moscow and took to the streets of other cities as well. In St. Petersburg, for example, people rushed to show support for mayor Anatoly Sobchak, who backed Yeltsin in the opposition to the coup. But the plotters were serious in their mission and they were not afraid, at least initially, to use force. On the night of August 20, armored personnel carriers moving toward the White House crushed three young men to death. But Yeltsin and his increasing crowd of supporters stood firm.

In the end, the Emergency Committee was unwilling to provoke more bloodshed. At 3 A.M., KGB chairman Vladimir Kruichkov, one of the members of the Emergency Committee, called Yeltsin to admit defeat. Gorbachev, returning to the capital, condemned the coup plotters, saying, "These people took advantage of the difficulties of the transitional period, and the tension in society and anxiety about what is going to happen to us, and decided to carry out far-fetched plans that would have plunged our society into utter turmoil."[97] He also noted that things had changed irreversibly. "I have come back . . . to another country, and I myself am a different man now."[98]

Yeltsin, showing his resolve and political adeptness to abort the coup, had clearly won the political spotlight. His leadership and courage throughout the event demon-

YELTSIN AND GORBACHEV

The political struggle between Gorbachev and Yeltsin grew increasingly tense in the late 1980s. When Yeltsin resigned from the Communist Party leadership in 1987 after criticizing both the Party and Gorbachev himself, Gorbachev, although angry and disappointed, purposely refused to condemn his former colleague. A balancing act between the two was just starting to take place and would develop into a political struggle between the Soviet Union and Russia. Yeltsin writes, in his autobiography, Against the Grain:

"It is my belief that if Gorbachev didn't have a Yeltsin, he would have had to invent one. Despite the dislike of me that he has shown recently, he realizes that he needs someone like me—prickly, sharp-tongued, the scourge of the overbureaucratized party apparat—and for this reason he keeps me near at hand. In this real-life production, the parts have been appropriately cast, as in a well-directed play. There is the conservative Ligachev, who plays the villain; there is Yeltsin, the bully boy, the madcap radical, and the wise, omniscient hero is Gorbachev himself. That, evidently, is how he sees it."

Citizens stand on a wall and cheer during the coup of 1991.

strated a real talent for motivating the Russian people and for outsmarting the coup plotters. He had masterminded plans to outwit them, using new technologies to communicate with the West despite the fact that the regular phone lines had been disconnected. In addition, he caused a state of confusion among the plotters themselves by leaking internal unconfirmed reports that some of them had resigned. According to Yeltsin biographer John Morrison, "Yeltsin's conduct during the coup displayed more than just courage; he not only outfaced but outsmarted the coup leaders, with a mixture of bluff and cunning."[99]

On August 24, Gorbachev resigned as the leader of the Soviet Communist Party. Only a few days later, the Party itself dissolved. Although Gorbachev continued to try to influence the future of the Soviet Union, he had lost credibility. In December, Yeltsin met with Leonid Kravchuk, from Ukraine, and Stanislav Shushkevich from Belarus to discuss the future of the union. They had not invited Gorbachev to the meeting. Together the three leaders signed a pact that announced the end of the USSR and the creation of the Commonwealth of Independent States in its place. One week later, accepting what had essentially already been decided without him, Gorbachev announced that the Soviet central government would cease to exist by the end of the year.

On Christmas Day 1991, Gorbachev called Bush to wish him a merry Christmas and to tell him that it was his last day in office. That night, the flag of the Soviet Union, with its red background and gold hammer and sickle, was lowered for the last time over the Kremlin. Although he had not wanted to abandon socialism and had resisted the breakup of the Soviet Union, Gorbachev spoke respectfully in January 1992 when he said, "I do not regard the end of the Cold War as a victory for one side. . . . The end of the Cold War is our common victory."[100]

Reflections on the Cold War

The Cold War was not a single military conflict but a political stalemate based on an ideological rivalry confounded by years of mistrust and suspicion. Despite the fact that many Americans in the initial post–Cold War years liked to boast that the United States "won" the Cold War, the Cold War was not a conflict that could be won or lost. In fact, most of its players, no matter how or where they finished in the end, paid a heavy price.

The Cold War, in practice, was a drawn-out military rivalry between two superpowers. Both the United States and the Soviet Union used terror and the threat of mass destruction to compete with one another and to maintain their power in the world. The competition between the two countries featured a spiraling arms race, whereby both the United States and the USSR had far more missiles than actually needed either for deterrence or self-defense.

The economic costs of the buildup are enormous. One estimate claims that as much as $8 trillion was spent worldwide on nuclear and other weapons from 1945 to 1996. According to Eduard Shevardnadze, as much as 50 percent of the Soviet Union's gross national product, or GNP, was spent on defense. Future costs of the

Cold War will include cleaning up nuclear weapon–based pollution. Estimates of this cost for the United States alone is somewhere between $100 and $400 billion.

These nuclear weapons sent the world to the brink of world annihilation on more than one occasion. Entire generations lived with the fear that any conflict or crisis might lead to a nuclear holocaust. Despite the American campaign to "duck and cover," a nuclear bomb would cause massive destruction. Some experts calculate that the amount of nuclear power amassed by the superpowers would be enough to destroy life on planet Earth several hundred times over. Although this terror, for the most part, has been lifted, rogue states such as Libya, North Korea, and Iraq may also now possess nuclear weapons and could one day again bring the world to the brink of a nuclear war, or further. This threat continues to cast a shadow over the post–Cold War world.

Countless conflicts were fought in the name of the Cold War. The United States, for its part, supported repressive regimes in El Salvador and Vietnam simply because they were "anticommunist." In many cases, these dictatorial regimes mistreated people and in no way subscribed to the American tenets of democracy and freedom, yet the United States supported them anyway. The Soviet Union behaved similarly, funding "procommunist" regimes in an attempt to stop "capitalist imperialism." In some cases, military know-how, ammunition, and vehicles supplied by the United States or the Soviet Union to Third World countries are now being used by rebel groups to support terrorist activities in the world. This poses a new and terrifying threat in the post–Cold War world.

In the many conflicts waged by both sides during the Cold War, hundreds of thousands of lives were lost. Bloody wars caused countless casualties and deaths as the superpowers faced off in places such as Korea, Vietnam, Afghanistan, Angola, Nicaragua, El Salvador, and Ethiopia, to name a few. Battles also caused enormous devastation to the places where they were fought; war ravaged entire cities and towns, and many countries are still struggling to revive their stagnating economies. In addition, lives were lost trying to cross the Berlin Wall, and in demonstrations in Eastern Europe and the Soviet Union. While some of these conflicts probably would have taken

Two Ukrainian military officials stand beside a nuclear missile that is to be destroyed.

THE FORMER SOVIET UNION

Arctic Ocean

Norwegian Sea

North Sea

Bering Sea

MOLDOVA LATVIA

KALININGRAD ESTONIA

White Sea Kara Sea

Magadan

LITHUANIA

BELARUS

Sea of Okhotsk

Moscow Nizhni Novgorod

Kiev

UKRAINE

RUSSIA

AZERBAIJAN

Novorossiysk

Black Sea

Lake Baikal

GEORGIA

Irkutsk

Vladivostok

UZBEKISTAN

Sea of Japan

KAZAKHSTAN

ARMENIA Caspian Sea Aral Sea Lake Balkhash Alma-Ata

Ashkhabad Tashkent Bishkek

TURKMENISTAN KYRGYZSTAN

Persian Gulf TAJIKISTAN Yellow Sea

Dushanbe

Independent Nations

place anyway, the Cold War made the struggles even more dire, often expanding the conflict and taking additional lives.

Ten years after the end of the Cold War, the United States is still grappling to find its place in the new world order. Participating actively in NATO and the UN, the United States has led peacekeeping efforts in places such as Somalia and Yugoslavia. It has spearheaded military conflict with Iraq, in an effort to drive Iraq out of its oil-rich neighbor, Kuwait.

But the role for the United States in the future is unclear. The Soviet Union, its main enemy in the Cold War, no longer exists. Russia and the other fourteen independent countries formed from the breakup of the Soviet Union have faced great challenges, including building new governments and political systems, and dealing with the economic decay inherited from decades of communism. The relationship between Russia and the United States will continue to be an important part of foreign policy in both countries. In recent years, the United States has rendered aid to Russia, Ukraine, and other new states, in an attempt to push these countries toward a Western model of democracy and a market economy. Whether Russia and other countries choose to follow this model or to forge a new path still remains to be seen.

Notes

Chapter 1: The Origins of the Cold War

1. Nicholas V. Riasanovsky, *A History of Russia*. New York: Oxford University Press, 1984, p. 457.

2. Vladimir Lenin, "A New Phase in the History of Russia Begins," April 15, 1917, in Brian MacArthur, ed., *Twentieth Century Speeches*. New York: Penguin Books, 1992, p. 58.

3. Quoted in Martin Walker, *The Cold War: A History*. New York: Henry Holt, 1993, p. 15.

4. Woodrow Wilson, "The World Must Be Made Safe for Democracy," in MacArthur, *Twentieth Century Speeches*, p. 56.

5. Quoted in Walker, *The Cold War*, p. 17.

6. Quoted in Stephen E. Ambrose, *Rise to Globalism: American Foreign Policy Since 1938*, 4th rev. ed. New York: Penguin Books, 1985, p. 58.

7. Quoted in Mary Beth Norton et al., *A People and a Nation: A History of the United States*. Boston: Houghton Mifflin, 1982, p. 793.

Chapter 2: Cold War Tensions Divide Europe

8. Quoted in Norton et al., *A People and a Nation*, p. 793.

9. Quoted in Jeremy Isaacs and Taylor Downing, *Cold War: An Illustrated History, 1945–1991*. Boston: Little, Brown, 1998, p. 17.

10. Ambrose, *Rise to Globalism*, p. 69.

11. Quoted in Isaacs and Downing, *Cold War*, p. 19.

12. Ambrose, *Rise to Globalism*, p. 71.

13. Quoted in Vladislav Zubok and Constantine Pleshakov, *Inside the Kremlin's Cold War: From Stalin to Khrushchev*. Cambridge, MA: Harvard University Press, 1996, p. 30.

14. Quoted in Isaacs and Downing, *Cold War*, p. 29.

15. Isaacs and Downing, *Cold War*, p. 35.

16. Quoted in Isaacs and Downing, *Cold War*, p. 30.

17. Quoted in Norton et al., *A People and a Nation*, p. 795.

18. Winston Churchill, "Iron Curtain Speech of March 5, 1946," archived at www.cnn.com/specialscold/war.

19. Harry S. Truman, "The Truman Doctrine" speech of March 12, 1947, in Richard Hofstadter and Beatrice Hofstadter, eds., *Great Issues in American History*, vol. 3. New York: Vintage Books, 1982, pp. 406–407.

20. George C. Marshall, "The Marshall Plan" speech on June 5, 1947, in Hofstadter and Hofstadter, *Great Issues in American History*, vol. 3, p. 410.

21. Quoted in Hofstadter and Hofstadter, *Great Issues in American History*, vol. 3, p. 410.

22. Quoted in Isaacs and Downing, *Cold War*, p. 50.

23. Quoted in Isaacs and Downing, *Cold War*, p. 52.

24. Michael Kort, *The Columbia Guide to the Cold War*. New York: Columbia University Press, 1998, p. 30.

25. Norton et al., *A People and a Nation*, p. 792.

Chapter 3: The Cold War Spreads to Asia

26. Quoted in Norton et al., *A People and a Nation*, p. 802.

27. Nikita Khrushchev, *Khrushchev Remembers: The Glasnost Tapes*. Boston: Little, Brown, 1990, p. 82.

28. Quoted in Norton et al., *A People and a Nation*, p. 803.

29. Quoted in Norton et al., *A People and a Nation*, p. 803.

30. Quoted in Isaacs and Downing, *Cold War*, p. 86.

31. Zubok and Pleshakov, *Inside the Kremlin's Cold War*, p. 57.

32. Quoted in Ambrose, *Rise to Globalism*, p. 113.

33. NSC-68: United States Objectives and Programs for National Security (April 14, 1950), www.mtholyoke.edu/acad/intrel/nsc-68/nsc68-1.htm.

34. Ambrose, *Rise to Globalism*, p. 114.

35. NSC-68, www.mtholyoke.edu/acad/intrel/nsc-68/nsc68-1.htm.

36. Quoted in Walker, *The Cold War*, p. 77.

37. Quoted in Dudley, *The Cold War*, p. 106.

38. Quoted in Zubok and Pleshakov, *Inside the Kremlin's Cold War*, p. 55.

39. Quoted in Zubok and Pleshakov, *Inside the Kremlin's Cold War*, p. 63.

40. Quoted in Zubok and Pleshakov, *Inside the Kremlin's Cold War*, p. 70.

Chapter 4: The Cold War at Home

41. Quoted in Norton et al., *A People and a Nation*, p. 851.

42. Quoted in National Archives Records Administration website, Records of the U.S. House of Representatives, www.nara.gov/nara/legislative/house_guide/hgch25bw.html.

43. Quoted in Norton et al., *A People and a Nation*, p. 852.

44. Quoted in the *New York Times*, October 29, 1992, B14, www.mdarchives.state.md.us/ecp/10/214/html/00010016.html.

45. Quoted in Walker, *The Cold War*, p. 70.

46. Quoted in Isaacs and Downing, *Cold War*, p. 109.

47. Excerpts from Joseph McCarthy, February 12, 1950 speech in Wheeling, West Virginia, www.cnn.com/specials/cold.war.

48. Excerpts from Joseph McCarthy, February 12, 1950 speech in Wheeling, West Virginia, www.cnn.com/specials/cold.war.

49. Telegram from Senator Joseph McCarthy to President Harry S. Truman, National Archives Records Administration website, www.nara.gov/education/cc/mccarthy.html.

50. Quoted in Isaacs and Downing, *Cold War*, pp. 114–15.

51. Internal Security Act of 1950, 64, Stat. 987 (1950), http://lawbooksusa.com/documents/internalsecurityact.htm.

52. Quoted in Dudley, *The Cold War*, pp. 102–103.

53. Quoted in Isaacs and Downing, *Cold War*, p. 115.

54. Quoted in Dudley, *The Cold War*, p. 103.

55. Quoted in Isaacs and Downing, *Cold War*, p. 116.

Chapter 5: New Leaders Provide a Possible Respite

56. Quoted in Norton et al., *A People and a Nation*, p. 855.

57. Quoted in Norton et al., *A People and a Nation*, p. 854.

58. Quoted in Norton et al., *A People and a Nation*, p. 855.

59. Ambrose, *Rise to Globalism*, p. 136.

60. John Foster Dulles, "Testimony on the Policy of Liberation," January 15, 1953, speech in Hofstadter and Hofstadter, *Great Issues in American History*, vol. 3, p. 431.

61. Quoted in Ambrose, *Rise to Globalism*, p. 139.

62. Quoted in Isaacs and Downing, *Cold War*, p. 134.

63. Quoted in Walker, *The Cold War*, p. 105.

64. Zubok and Pleshakov, *Inside the Kremlin's Cold War*, p. 185.

65. Quoted in Isaacs and Downing, *Cold War*, p. 139.

66. Quoted in Norton et al., *A People and a Nation*, p. 894.

67. Quoted in Zubok and Pleshakov, *Inside the Kremlin's Cold War*, p. 189.

68. Quoted in Zubok and Pleshakov, *Inside the Kremlin's Cold War*, p. 189.

Chapter 6: Cold War Nightmares: Tensions Escalate

69. Quoted in Hofstadter and Hofstadter, *Great Issues in American History*, vol. 3, p. 546.

70. Quoted in Norton et al., *A People and a Nation*, p. 897.

71. Khrushchev, *Khrushchev Remembers*, p. 165.

72. Quoted in Norton et al., *A People and a Nation*, p. 899.

73. Khrushchev, *Khrushchev Remembers*, p. 171.

74. Quoted in Edwin O. Guthman and Jeffrey Shulman, eds., *Robert Kennedy, In His Own Words*. New York: Bantam, 1988, pp. 394–95.

Chapter 7: Détente and After

75. Quoted in Hofstadter and Hofstadter, *Great Issues in American History*, vol. 3, pp. 564–65.

76. Quoted in Isaacs and Downing, *Cold War*, p. 289.

77. Quoted in Kort, *The Columbia Guide to the Cold War*, p. 67.

78. Quoted in Hofstadter and Hofstadter, *Great Issues in American History*, vol. 3, pp. 573–74.

79. Quoted in Kort, *The Columbia Guide to the Cold War*, p. 72.

80. Quoted in Kort, *The Columbia Guide to the Cold War*, p. 73.

81. Excerpts from Ronald Reagan, Address to the Nation on Defense and National Security, March 23, 1983, www.cnn.com/specials/cold.war.

82. Quoted in Walker, *The Cold War*, p. 268.

83. Quoted in Norton et al., *A People and a Nation*, p. 919.

84. Quoted in Kort, *The Columbia Guide to the Cold War*, p. 78.

85. Quoted in Walker, *The Cold War*, p. 276.

Chapter 8: The Cold War Comes to a Close

86. Quoted in Isaacs and Downing, *Cold War*, p. 355.

87. Isaacs and Downing, *Cold War*, p. 356.

88. Quoted in Isaacs and Downing, *Cold War*, p. 359.

89. Excerpts from Gorbachev's Speech to the United Nations, December 7, 1988, www.cnn.com/specials/cold.war.

90. Isaacs and Downing, *Cold War*, p. 376.

91. Quoted in Isaacs and Downing, *Cold War*, p. 382.

92. Quoted in Isaacs and Downing, *Cold War*, p. 387.

93. Quoted in Isaacs and Downing, *Cold War*, p. 387.

94. Quoted in Kort, *The Columbia Guide to the Cold War*, p. 87.

95. Isaacs and Downing, *Cold War*, p. 401.

96. Yeltsin address of August, 19, 1991, www.cnn.com/specials/cold.war.

97. Excerpt from Gorbachev's Address after the Coup, August 22, 1991, www.cnn.com/specials/cold.war.

98. Quoted in Isaacs and Downing, *Cold War*, p. 416.

99. John Morrison, *Boris Yeltsin: From Bolshevik to Democrat*. New York: Dutton, 1991, p. 284.

100. Quoted in Isaacs and Downing, *Cold War*, p. 417.

For Further Reading

Stephen Goode, *The End of Détente?: U.S.-Soviet Relations*. New York: Franklin Watts, 1981.

Michael G. Kort, *The Cold War*. Brookfield, CT: Millbrook Press, 1994.

Michael Kort, *Mikhail Gorbachev*. New York: Franklin Watts, 1990.

John Pimlott, *The Cold War: Conflict in the 20th Century*. New York: Franklin Watts, 1987.

Michael A. Schuman, *Harry S. Truman*. Springfield, NJ: Enslow, 1997.

James A. Warren. *Cold War: The American Crusade Against World Communism, 1945–91*. New York: Lothrop, Lee, & Shepard, 1996.

David K. Wright, *War in Vietnam*. Chicago: Childrens Press, 1989.

Works Consulted

Stephen E. Ambrose, *Rise to Globalism: American Foreign Policy Since 1938*, 4th rev. ed. New York: Penguin Books, 1983. Provides a revisionist overview of American foreign policy since 1938.

William Dudley, ed., *The Cold War: Opposing Viewpoints*. San Diego: Greenhaven Press, 1992. This book is a good resource that presents speeches and debates of U.S. policy makers and others from the Cold War on both sides of a given issue.

John Lewis Gaddis, *We Now Know: Rethinking Cold War History*. Oxford: Oxford University Press, 1997. Gaddis uses recently available documents to look back at the Cold War. He places most of the responsibility on Stalin and the Soviet Union.

Edwin O. Guthman and Jeffrey Shulman, eds., *Robert Kennedy, In His Own Words: The Unpublished Recollections of the Kennedy Years*. New York: Bantam, 1988. This book contains published transcripts of interviews with Robert Kennedy originally recorded in the mid-1960s for the John F. Kennedy Library.

Richard Hofstadter and Beatrice K. Hofstadter, eds., *Great Issues in American History, From Reconstruction to the Present Day, 1864–1981*. vol. 3. New York: Vintage Books, 1982. This book includes significant documents and speeches in American history.

Jeremy Isaacs and Taylor Downing, *Cold War: An Illustrated History, 1945–1991*. Boston: Little, Brown, 1998. This is a comprehensive overview written as a companion to the CNN television series. The book is complete with pictures, firsthand accounts, and interesting sidebars.

George F. Kennan, *Russia and the West Under Lenin and Stalin*. Boston: Little, Brown, 1961. The author of the famous "long telegram" that served to shape the U.S. policy of containment takes a look at the relationship between the Soviet Union and Western countries from 1917 to the end of World War II.

Paul Kennedy, *The Rise and Fall of the Great Powers*. New York: Oxford University Press, 1984. Kennedy examines the changing balance of power in the world from the sixteenth century through 1981. Much attention is given to the Cold War and the rise of a bipolar world.

Nikita Khrushchev, *Khrushchev Remembers: The Glasnost Tapes*. Boston: Little, Brown, 1990. Khrushchev dictated these candid memoirs in his last years.

Michael Kort, *The Columbia Guide to the Cold War*. New York: Columbia University Press, 1998. An invaluable reference on the Cold War, this guide gives an overview of the main events and issues, an encyclopedia of topics and important figures, a chronology of events, and a thorough bibliography of resources on all subjects concerning the Cold War.

Brian MacArthur, ed., *The Penguin Book of Twentieth Century Speeches*. New York: Penguin Books, 1992. Includes great speeches from famous politicians and others.

John Morrison, *Boris Yeltsin: From Bolshevik to Democrat*. New York: Dutton, 1991. Written by a former Reuters Moscow bureau chief, this book examines Yeltsin's political career up to 1991.

Mary Beth Norton, et al., *A People and a Nation: A History of the United States*. Boston: Houghton Mifflin, 1982. The authors provide survey of American history.

R. R. Palmer and Joel Colton, *A History of the Modern World*. New York: Knopf, 1995. Gives a lengthy and in-depth account of world history.

David Remnick, *Lenin's Tomb: The Last Days of the Soviet Empire*. New York: Random House, 1993. A former Moscow correspondent for *The Washington Post* provides a look at Soviet life, people, and leaders from 1986 to 1991.

Nicholas V. Riasanovsky, *A History of Russia*. New York: Oxford University Press, 1984. This book is the authoritative source on Russian history.

Werner Sikorski and Rainer Laabs, *Checkpoint Charlie and the Wall: A Divided People Rebel*. Berlin: Ullstein Buchverlage GmbH, 2000. The authors have collected stories and pictures from the Berlin Wall.

Alexis de Tocqueville, *Democracy in America*. Garden City, NY: Doubleday, 1969. This view of American politics and government was written in 1832.

Adam B. Ulam, *Expansion and Coexistence: Soviet Foreign Policy 1917–83*. New York: Praeger, 1974. Provides an analysis of the ideology and figures that shaped the foreign policy of the Soviet Union.

Martin Walker, *The Cold War: A History*. New York: Henry Holt, 1993. A British journalist who worked as a correspondent for the *Manchester Guardian* in Moscow in the 1980s gives a comprehensive account of the Cold War.

J. Robert Wegs, *Europe Since 1945: A Concise History*. New York: St. Martin's Press, 1984. This book examines European politics after World War II.

Boris Yeltsin, *Against the Grain: An Autobiography*. New York: Summit Books, 1990. Russia's first president tells his story.

Boris Yeltsin, *The Struggle for Russia*. New York: Random House, 1994. Russia's first president gives an inside account of Russia's journey toward democracy.

Vladislav Zubok and Constantine Pleshakov, *Inside the Kremlin's Cold War: From Stalin to Khrushchev*. Cambridge, MA: Harvard University Press, 1996.

The authors, Russian historians, provide a first-of-its-kind, scholarly look at the Cold War using newly opened Soviet archives.

Websites

CNN Interactive Site on the Cold War, http://www.cnn.com/specials/cold.war.

Cold War International History Project website at the Woodrow Wilson International Center for Scholars, http://cwihp.si.edu.

Internal Security Act of 1950, 64, Stat. 987 (1950), http://lawbooksusa.com/documents/internalsecurityact.htm.

Library of Congress website, http://www.loc.gov.homepage/lchp.html.

National Archives Records Administration website, http://www.nara.gov

National Security Archive, http://www.gwu.edu/~nsarchiv/.

New York Times, October 29, 1992, B14, http://www.mdarchives.state.md.us/ecp/10/214/html/00010016.html.

Internet Sources

"Eisenhower's Domino Speech," http:www.uiowa.edu/~c030162/common/handouts.

NSC-68: United States Objectives and Programs for National Security (April 14, 1950). www.mtholyoke.edu/acad/intrel/nsc-68/nsc68-1.htm.

Index

Picture Credits

Cover photo: Courtesy Ronald Reagan Library

© Bettmann/CORBIS, 19, 55 (top), 57, 62, 66, 67, 96

© CORBIS, 15

© Larry Downing/Woodfin Camp and Associates, 100

© John Ficara/Woodfin Camp and Associates, 91, 94

© Hulton/Archive by Getty Images, 23, 28, 32, 43 (top and bottom), 48, 55 (bottom), 56, 59, 65, 69, 70, 73, 77, 83, 86, 87, 90, 91, 93, 95, 99, 109

© Hulton-Deutsch Collection/CORBIS, 14

Library of Congress, 17, 21, 30, 34, 49, 50, 64, 82, 88

© Jeff Lowenthal/Woodfin Camp and Associates, 89

© Robert Maass/CORBIS, 105

NASA, 76

National Archives, 22, 114

© Photoassist/Woodfin Camp and Associates, 38

Reuters/Mikhail Chernichkin/Hulton/Archive, 113

Reuters/Charles Platiau/Hulton/Archive, 103

Reuters/Stinger/Archive Photos, 107

Ronald Reagan Library, 97

© Scheufler Collection/CORBIS, 13

© Tom Stoddart/Katz Pictures, 10

© David & Peter Turnley/CORBIS, 106, 111

© Underwood & Underwood/CORBIS, 18

U.S. Army/Harry S. Truman Library, 42

About the Author

Britta Bjornlund's keen interest in the relationship between the Soviet Union and the United States originated in high school when she began learning Russian and traveled to the Soviet Union for the first time. Currently a program manager at the Center for Russian Leadership Development at the Library of Congress, she holds a master's degree in international relations from the Johns Hopkins University School of Advanced International Studies (SAIS) and a bachelor's degree from Williams College.

Ms. Bjornlund has worked as an advisor to various government agencies throughout the former Soviet Union, and she witnessed the fall of the USSR firsthand in 1991. She lives in Washington D.C. with her cat Trotsky, and is an avid fan of the Washington Capitals ice hockey team.